LEGAL
LYNCHING

LEGAL LYNCHING

RACISM, INJUSTICE

AND THE DEATH PENALTY

REV. JESSE JACKSON

WITH JESSE JACKSON, Jr.

MARLOWE & COMPANY

First Marlowe & Company edition, 1996

Published by
Marlowe & Company
632 Broadway, Seventh Floor
New York, NY 10012

This book published in association with National Press Books.

The publisher thanks the Death Penalty Information Center (DPIC) in
Washington, D.C. for providing material, research, and assistance for this
book. Without the assistance of DPIC, this book would not have been
possible.

Designed by Michael Mendelsohn

Manufactured in the United States of America

Library of Congress Cataloging-in-Publication Data

Jackson, Jesse, 1941-
    Legal lynching : racism, injustice, and the death penalty / by Jesse
Jackson. — 1st ed.
        p.   cm.
    Includes bibliographical references.
    ISBN 1-56924-761-7
    1. Capital punishment—United States. 2. Discrimination in capital
punishment—United States. 3. Discrimination in criminal justice administration—United States. 4. United States—Race relations.
5. Afro-Americans. I. Title.
HV8699.U5J33   1996
365.6'6'0973—dc20   96-18842
                                                            CIP

This book is dedicated to the principle of equal protection under the law for all Americans contained in the Fourteenth Amendment to the Constitution, and to the innocent Americans who have been wrongly executed or imprisoned in violation of the principle. It is also dedicated to the people and organizations who are working to abolish the death penalty and break the cycle of violence that plagues our country.

CONTENTS

ACKNOWLEDGMENTS

I would like to thank a number of people who were very important to the development of this book. Frank Watkins was instrumental in creating the concept for the book and doing research for several chapters, and contributed mightily during the writing. Joel Joseph at National Press Books was one of the first to see the need for this volume, and provided inspiration for the project. Denis Gaynor and John McFarlane, also of National Press Books, provided excellent research on several chapters. The aid of Rick MacArthur and Richard Dieter of the Death Penalty Information Center was essential to the project's success, as were the editorial skills of Robert Weisser. John Weber of Marlowe & Company helped immensely in bringing the book to the public. Also of invaluable assistance has been Theresa Caldwell, press secretary for the National Rainbow Coalition.

LEGAL LYNCHING

INTRODUCTION

In the middle of the night I am awakened by a pounding at the door. When I answer the door, half-asleep, I am confronted by unrelenting police officers who arrest me and take me to a police station. There, alone and frightened, I am interrogated through the night, and when morning arrives, I am charged with a serious crime. "You are mistaken," I say. "I am innocent. I have never seen this man you tell me I have murdered. I was not even in this city the day he was killed." But no one listens, and I am abandoned on death row, proclaiming my innocence to the uncaring walls.

I wake up then, usually in a cold sweat, with a vague sensation that I have just returned from a foreign country where human rights are disregarded or have no standing, where the world cannot or will not do anything to help me. But I know that this nightmare is a living reality in my own country for scores and possibly hundreds of Americans on death row. The innocents are black, white, Hispanic—all races, and all types of men and women. They may be victims of racism, poor legal work, incompetent judges. They are the walking dead.

For more than ten years, Clarence Brandley was one of the walking dead. Before his incarceration, Brandley was 28 years old and a hard-working janitor in a Conroe, Texas high school, an hour's drive from Houston. One hot summer morning a blond teenage girl was brutally raped and murdered in the school, and Brandley, the only black janitor, became the sole target of the investigation. In fact, the investigating police officer told Brandley and another janitor, "One of the two of you is going to hang for this." Turning to Brandley he said, "Since you're the nigger, you're elected."

Despite this daunting threat, Brandley affirmed his innocence. A lie detector test confirmed the truth of his statements. There was no solid evidence against him—no fingerprints, no blood, no DNA, no hair. The government, however, would not be denied. The prosecutor manipulated the jury pool so that he could argue his case before an all-white jury, screaming before them at one point that Brandley was a murderer and a rapist and that he should be convicted and sentenced to death in order to protect society. All but one of the jurors bought the prosecutor's fear-mongering histrionics, and the result was a hung jury.

The prosecutor did not give up, and retried Brandley for rape and murder, again striking all black jurors from

14

the jury pool. (Unlike what the world saw in the O.J. Simpson case, it is usually the prosecutor who can control who is chosen for the jury.) This time the jury, with the judge's approval, convicted Brandley and sentenced him to die in the electric chair.

Brandley was confined to a bare cell in a cold Texas prison. A fortunate turn of events on the outside brought his case into the public eye. A competent lawyer discovered that the prosecutor had failed to turn over to the defense substantial evidence that Brandley was indeed innocent, and *Sixty Minutes* did a segment on him. After ten years on death row, Brandley's conviction was overturned.

We have always had two systems of justice in America, one for the wealthy and one for the poor. We have also always had a double standard in the criminal justice system, one for whites and one for people of color. The gravest injustices occur when a poor man or woman is wrongfully charged with a capital offense and sentenced to death. Wrongful convictions can be overturned, but wrongful executions can never be undone. Judges and juries are human—they make mistakes, and innocent people may be killed. Only God can create life, and so man has no right to take life. I believe that the commandment "Thou shalt not kill" applies to judges and juries as well as to everyone else.

Yet Republicans and Democrats alike want to cut off the appeals of those on death row. "It costs too much money," they shout. In other words, American citizens get all the justice they can afford. Had these proposals been law when Clarence Brandley was on death row, he would be dead. Innocent, but dead. Streamlined appeals will absolutely guarantee that we will continue to execute innocent men, women, and children. What is the price tag on that?

Statistics show that the death penalty does not deter crime. Revenge, then, becomes the reason for capital punishment. When the government executes a prisoner, all of us have blood on our hands, and death hangs heavily on our minds. How can we teach our children that killing and revenge are evils, and then have our elected representatives kill and seek revenge?

Whether because of campaign rhetoric or the fears of citizens, our nation seems to have gone death penalty mad. New York is the latest state to reimpose the death penalty, even though the number of killings in Manhattan, long considered a jurisdiction with a high murder rate, decreased from 648 in 1975 to half that in 1994 while the state had no death penalty. And the federal government is broadening the number of crimes in which the death penalty may be applied, and is prosecuting a growing number of capital cases.

While many politicians argue that we have become a color-blind society, the Rodney King and O.J. Simpson trials have placed race and racial justice front and center in the American political debate. In terms of justice, we are not color-blind. Many white police officers behave differently than most black police officers and certainly see things through a different set of lenses. Most white jurors see facts differently than do black jurors. The nationwide debate following the Simpson verdict verified this—blacks and whites view the criminal justice system from two different vantage points. Whites see it from the top down. Blacks see it from the bottom up. Whites see it as working. Blacks see it as stacked against them, working against their interests, oppressing them. Whites see the criminal justice system as essentially color-blind. Blacks see it as essentially discriminatory toward people of color.

One conclusion that we can all draw from the Simpson case—and I think more and more people are recognizing this—is that a wealthy defendant gets more justice than a poor one. And that is one of the most significant problems with the death penalty. Those who are sentenced to death usually have had mediocre representation—usually one overworked and underpaid lawyer from the public defender's office, not a dream team of lawyers, jury consultants, and the best expert witnesses money can buy. High-priced lawyers are not clustering around indigent defendants, jostling each other to get another case from a client who can't pay. Very often, lawyers have to be cajoled into taking these cases for a pittance that guarantees they will provide minimal defense.

Can we as a nation afford to condemn poor murder defendants to death? Is that what America stands for? "Equal justice under law," the words carved into the white marble facade of the U.S. Supreme Court building, is the guiding principle of American law. But more of us realize that American justice is equal only for those who can afford it. American justice, like American medical care, is the best in the world for those able to pay for it.

While Clarence Brandley got sterling outside assistance (there were massive demonstrations in his support, and such organizations as Amnesty International joined his cause), most residents of death row have no outside champions. That Brandley's life was finally saved does not prove that justice in America is working. It only demonstrates that when the world is watching, justice is possible. This means that in the dark shadows of death row, hundreds of innocent people will die. The Death Penalty Information Center (DPIC) of Washington, D.C. has documented 23 cases in which innocent defendants have been executed. Certainly there are dangerous criminals in America who do not deserve ever to live outside of prison walls. But we can keep these dangerous prisoners incarcerated until they die, or until they become harmless to society.

It often seems that we still impose the death sentence in the United States for purely political reasons. Politicians, including President Clinton, support the death penalty to show that they are tough on crime. But you can be tough on crime and still oppose the death penalty. Bronx (New York) District Attorney Robert Johnson, who has an outstanding reputation for being tough on crime not only in his home borough but amongst his colleagues in other jurisdictions, refuses to seek the death penalty in any case in which the ultimate punishment is an option. He knows the system all too well and cannot tolerate the possibility of condemning an innocent man or woman to death. Johnson once prosecuted—and won conviction for—a man who was later proven to be innocent. That memory has made this tough prosecutor an advocate for eliminating capital punishment. Johnson remains opposed even though George Pataki, the new governor of New York who reinstated the death penalty, has threatened him with removal from office.

Johnson is not alone. Twenty-year veteran Manhattan District Attorney Robert Morgenthau is a staunch, vocal, public opponent of the death penalty. He argues convincingly that the death penalty hinders the fight against crime by draining resources from other avenues of criminal prosecution. "Promoted by members of both political parties in response to an angry populace," Morgenthau has said, "capital punishment is a mirage that distracts society from more fruitful, less facile answers. It extracts a terrible price in dollars, lives and human decency. Rather than tamping down the flames of violence, it fuels them while draining millions of dollars from more promising efforts to restore safety to our lives." Because opposition to the death penalty appears to be unpopular with the general public (although I will demonstrate that this idea is not as fixed as it seems), most district attorneys (who are elected officials) and prosecutors keep quiet about the death penalty. That two leading New York DAs would go public in opposition to the death penalty is strong evidence that it is not working, will not work, and is contrary to the interests of justice and a civilized society.

While the United States is technologically and economically one of the most advanced nations in the world, it can also be said to be one of the most uncivilized. We are one of the few nations that allow teenagers to be executed for their crimes. Joining us in those ranks are Nigeria, Saudi Arabia, Iraq, Iran, Pakistan, and Yemen, associates which are often criticized internationally for their human rights violations. Nearly every one of these other countries is a dictatorship known for cruel treatment of prisoners and lack of due process, fairness, and justice.

Of the Western democracies, the United States stands alone in using, let alone increasing, the use of the death penalty as a means of punishment. This bucks the trend of civilization, which for centuries has been decreasing the use of capital punishment. Some will argue that we cannot be guided by what other countries do since the United States is an astoundingly violent nation. After all, nearly 25,000 Americans are murdered every year. But having the state murder hundreds more is not the answer.

Violence begets violence, and by endorsing the death penalty, we as a nation are perpetuating the cycle of violence. We are telling our citizens that murder can be justified, because the government does it. But the government should be striving to break the cycle of violence, not to perpetuate it.

Many people all over the world believe that the death penalty is the ultimate human rights violation. All European nations have abolished the death penalty. Israel, at least officially, abides by the commandment "Thou shalt not kill." The laws of Israel do not allow the death penalty to avenge even President Rabin's assassination. Recently, South Africa ruled that the death penalty was unconstitutional under its new constitution, which strongly reflects American constitutional values. The new South Africa has adopted our ban against cruel punishments, using it to outlaw capital punishment. If Israel and South Africa, which have suffered from so much violence, can control vengeance and stop the cycle of death, then the United States can do so as well.

We are not a backward people. We are a progressive and helpful people, when armed with the truth. If we see that people are starving in Somalia, we want to help with food, money, and medical aid. If there is an earthquake in Japan, we are the first to offer assistance.

We claim that we advance the cause of human rights

around the world. But capital punishment is a human rights issue and on this issue we lag behind the world community.

When I travel abroad and speak out to protest human rights abuses in other countries, I am often confronted with our own abuses, tops among them being racism and the death penalty. To lead the world America must have moral authority. We do not. One of the weakest links in our moral armor is our resort to legal executions.

In this book, I shall discuss how we can fix that weakest link. I will show the place of state-sanctioned killing in history, and the strides the people of the earth have made to eradicate it. I will explain why we no longer need the death penalty, and the strict alternative sentences that we already have that can replace it. I will investigate the undue burden that capital punishment places on poor people, on minorities, and on those who have no voice in our society. I will outline the moral, ethical, and religious arguments against capital punishment. And I will end with a message of hope that America will soon be joining the rest of the civilized world in moving toward a death penalty-free future.

This book is about life and death, black and white, rich and poor, justice and injustice, innocence and guilt. It is about who lives and who dies, and how we decide who lives and who dies. It is also about justice for all of us. For whenever an innocent man is put to death it kills a little part of each one of us—it makes us all a little more insensitive to life and death. When the government kills, we are all executioners. Let us join the family of nations of the world and put an end, once and for all, to the barbaric and inhumane practice of killing people in the name of law and justice.

The only possible justification for the death penalty is vengeance, but the Lord says, "Vengeance is mine." The government should not be in the business of revenge. Justice, not revenge, is the proper role for government. The death penalty is unjust, first because it is morally wrong, but also because it is unevenly and unfairly implemented, discriminatorily enforced against the weak, the poor, and minorities. I call for the abolition of the death penalty in the United States in all cases, even when the accused desires it. As I will show, we have more than enough cost-effective options in our legal arsenal to keep murderers out of society for the rest of their lives.

Who would want revenge more than Coretta Scott King, the wife of Dr. Martin Luther King, Jr.? But she knew that adding violence to violence would not bring relief:

> Although my husband was assassinated and my mother-in-law was murdered, I refuse to accept the cynical judgment that their killers deserve to be executed. To do so would perpetuate the tragic cycle of violence that feeds itself. It would be a disservice to all that my husband and his mother lived for and believed.

Let us stop the killing. Thou shalt not kill—that is my beacon. It is now time to stop the violence, in our streets, in our courtrooms, in our prisons, in our statehouses and governors' mansions, as well as in Congress, the White House, and the Supreme Court. It is time to join the growing chorus around the world that humanity can no longer tolerate the death penalty.

1

THE ROOTS OF
CAPITAL PUNISHMENT

A convicted killer mounts a tall horse, and has his hands bound behind his back. The horse is led beneath a mighty tree, where a well-crafted noose is tossed over the strongest branch. The man on the horse looks beseechingly at the small audience assembled to watch him die. Most of the congregation stands silently, expectantly. One bold person says, "Die, Dodd."

The swinging rope slaps the man in the face. When asked if he has any last words, he says, "I'm sorry. I repent. Lord forgive these people." The executioner roughly pushes a black sack over the man's head and pulls the noose around his neck. At a nod from the official in charge, the executioner smacks the horse on its haunches.

The man appears to jump backward as his mount leaves him. For an instant, he seems to be floating in air, but then his body is jolted by the tightening rope wrapped around his throat. The witnesses hear an ugly crack as his neck snaps, and he shakes violently for a few moments. His bowels and bladder empty simultaneously. The executioner smiles inwardly at his efficient handiwork, and the audience feels charged with a near-sexual exhilaration at having seen the life taken from this man.

Most of us have watched this scene in western movies without connecting it to our modern, civilized nation. We no longer hang cattle rustlers or bandits after a kangaroo court. We have supposedly advanced far beyond the old frontier justice, and now have a strong but fair rehabilitative criminal justice system. For capital crimes, our progress since Wild West times can be attributed to one basic principle.

We don't use the horse anymore.

The blood-frenzied murder described above, with the exception of the unwitting animal, could have been the execution of Westley Allan Dodd in Washington State on January 5, 1993—the first legal hanging in the United States since 1965. The pastor of the Walla Walla prison rightly noted in an article on the event, "If this execution of Westley Allan Dodd by the State of Washington were not in its essence an act of barbarism, there would not have been more than 100 reporters waiting to see if they would be chosen by lottery to serve as one of the 12 official witnesses of the actual execution."

History will condemn the United States for this murder and hundreds more like it. The world has watched America purportedly reach the pinnacle of humanitarian progress over its more than two centuries of existence. Founded on enlightened democratic ideals, America prescribes justice for its citizens and for the world. To live in this country is supposedly to have left the ancient, blood-loving cultures of the past behind in favor of a more advanced society.

THE DEATH PENALTY IN HISTORY

Capital punishment has history and tradition on its side. Jesus himself was the victim of capital punishment. Thus, one reason capital punishment is so difficult to outlaw as an unacceptable human practice is that its roots are deep in the human psyche, in tradition, and in the evolution of the practice of law.

After nearly 4,000 years of documented capital punishment for crimes ranging from insult to treason, the last two decades has seen country after country abolish the death penalty. The United States remains in the undistinguished company of nearly 100 other executioner-states, including China, Saudi Arabia, Iraq, and Vietnam.

As the following death penalty retrospective will attest, the history of state-sanctioned execution is a sordid one brimming with inhuman and misguided justice. Despite the fact that capital punishment has never been proven to deter criminals, and that this grisly form of public retribution has been long outdated, the United States not only still condones this barbaric prac-

27

tice as a rational form of discipline, but is expanding the number of crimes subject to capital punishment and increasing the number of people subject to this barbaric practice.

Thirty-eight centuries ago, King Hammurabi of Babylon prescribed a code of 282 "laws," some of which mandated death for 25 different crimes. Despite its use of capital punishment, this law code was remarkably forward-thinking: it advanced the rights of women and children thousands of years before Western countries did, and made punishment something for the state—not the aggrieved party—to carry out. In Babylon, women were treated with honor and shared many legal rights with men. Article 142 of Hammurabi's Code, for example, proclaimed that "If a woman has hated her husband and states 'thou shalt not have (the natural use of) me,'. . . , that woman shall suffer no punishment; she may take her dowry and go to her father's house." Such a law was far more progressive than American law in the 1800s, or even the present laws in present-day Babylon (Iraq).

Despite the civility embedded in the code, modern society generally considers the punishments of Hammurabi to have been extremely harsh. For instance, the first article stated, "If a man has accused a man of manslaughter and then has not proved it against him, the accuser shall be put to death" and a later article prescribed the death penalty for "sorcerers." Today, the former seems brutal and the latter seems superfluous. But the Salem witch trials on our own shores took place only a few hundred years ago. Which then is the more brutal society?

The first documented death sentence was handed down in Egypt in the sixteenth century before Christ, though it is almost certain that there had been many others before this. (Ancient Chinese writings make numerous references to beheadings before this time.) The unlucky Egyptian criminal was guilty of "magic" and was allowed to select his own method of death.

Death as discipline continued to flourish in the ancient world, reaching its zenith around 700 B.C., when Dracon of Athens designed and implemented a code of laws whereby every crime was punishable by execution. Thus the origin of the term *draconian*.

Two centuries later, the Roman Republic's Law of the Twelve Tablets called for the death of certain criminals, though distinctions were made based on the offender's social class. An execution was carried out, for instance, only if the accused were a slave or if the victim were a freeman, and the punishment usually involved the guilty party being thrown from a rock. Even making a disturbance in the city at night was punishable by death, and vestal virgins who violated their vows of chastity were buried alive. Other laws around this time drew upon more nefarious means of quenching man's savage blood thirst, including beheading, hanging, crucifixion, burning alive, and stoning. Even the ancient Jews, who suffered in modern times at the hands of Hitler and other dictators, practiced cruel punishment against those conquered in Palestine, including starvation, pouring molten lead on the offender, tearing the criminal to death with red-hot pincers, or sawing the victim asunder.

The Roman Empire, whose executions included that of Jesus Christ, impaled most criminals or beat them to death. Parricides—people who murdered their father or mother—would be bound in a sack with a dog, a rooster, and a snake, and then thrown into water. This bizarre practice continued in some places until the Middle Ages.

In Europe, the Church and a number of great rulers such as William the Conqueror opposed the death penalty. But by medieval times, executions became more indiscriminate, and torture often accompanied death. The number of capital crimes increased, too; in England, for example, a death writ condemning heretics to burn or drown lasted from 1382 to 1677. French nobles at least had the comfort of knowing they would be honorably beheaded with an axe rather than being hung or drawn and quartered—often how members of the lower classes would meet their demise. Women were usually strangled to death and burned to ashes out of a sense of "decency" to their sex. (It would have been improper to have a woman's bare limbs, whether attached to her body or otherwise, as a public spectacle. Later, Henry VIII made boiling to death a legal form of execution, and over 72,000 of his subjects were killed by this and other means. By the seventeenth century, no less than 200,000 women had been executed as witches, and in 1818, people were killed for attempting to use forged money. Bodies were left on display for weeks and sometimes months as governments' practice of capital punishment escalated.

These executions were public affairs, because the governments hoped to arouse a fear of punishment in the populace and so deter crime. Of course, this strategy has never been proven to work. While casual infractions may be reduced or eliminated if the offender knows he will be immediately electrocuted, most murders are "crimes of passion"—usually committed out of rage or hatred—in which the criminal never considers the consequences. The great fanfare given executions caused an almost carnival atmosphere at the site, and people would come for the thrill of it, not for the moral lessons to be learned.

Take, for example, the case of Robert-Francois Damiens. Convicted of attempting to assassinate King Louis XV in 1757, Damiens was sentenced to death by the following decree:

> The Court declares Robert-Francois Damiens duly convicted of the crime . . . and further the Court orders that he then be taken to the Greve, and, on a scaffold erected for the purpose, that his chest, arms, thighs and calves be burnt with pincers; his right hand, holding the knife with which he committed the said parricide, burnt in sulfur; that boiling oil, melted lead, and rosin and wax mixed with sulfur be poured into his wounds;

31

and after that his body be pulled and dismembered by four horses, and the members and body consumed in fire, and the ashes scattered to the winds. . . .

Damiens had knicked the King with a knife (the monarch's royal furs blunted most of the attack), but his sentence reflected something else: an animalistic sense of vengeance in the French people. The sentence was carried out before mobs of excited men, women, and children, who gathered in the plaza and on rooftops to watch the torture and to see the horses tear his body asunder. The people actually got more than was advertised, for the horses were unsuccessful in three tries to rip the failed assassin limb from limb, and his arms and legs were ultimately hacked from his body with an axe. In the midst of what was considered at that time to be the pinnacle of civilization, the primitive lust for blood had risen up and consumed the population.

OPPOSITION TO
STATE-SANCTIONED EXECUTIONS

Prior to the eighteenth century in Europe, there was nearly unanimous opinion that society needed the death penalty and torture of criminals to keep lawlessness from growing beyond all bounds. But exhibitions like the Damiens execution and growing moral concerns caused a small opposition to form.

In 1764, the Italian philosopher and economist Cesare Beccaria almost singlehandedly began the modern crusade against torture and the death penalty by publishing *Essays on Crimes and Punishments*. Soon, others joined him, and a small movement began to grow throughout Europe and North America to reform the criminal justice system by eliminating torture and capital punishment. Initially, only religious groups already known for their pacifism supported this movement. It would be centuries—and only after the development of the modern social sciences—that the mainline churches and their theologians and ethicists would join in the debate over curbing the death penalty.

Beccaria began his crusade at a time when, in the West, governments were increasing the number of offenses punishable by death. Beccaria could see the practical justification for capital punishment during times of civil unrest or social disorder or to prevent a revolution; though, in times of peace, he recognized that its only justification was if it served as a deterrent to crime. Even so, he wrote that his study of the history of penal law had convinced him that the death penalty had never worked as a deterrent of any sort. Modern social science has come to the same conclusion, even though deterrence remains a significant rationale for capital punishment in the United States.

The arguments that Beccaria put forth in the mid-1700s are still at the heart of the debate today. He claimed that long-term imprisonment is as effective in prevent-

ing crime as is the death penalty; that the state's partici-
pation in capital punishment increases rather than
decreases violence in society; and that the death penalty's
finality leaves no room for corrective action if the person
is later found to be innocent.

The anti-death penalty movement gained popularity
among those who embraced the philosophical tenets of
the period known as the Enlightenment, where rational-
ity and science were predominant. Its first effect was to
reduce the number of crimes punishable by death.

In England, Sir Samuel Romilly and Jeremy Bentham
championed arguments similar to Beccaria's. Romilly
took these arguments to Parliament and began to push for
laws restricting capital punishment. He had some
successes; for example, in 1808, Parliament abolished the
death penalty for pickpockets.

Romilly died in 1818, but the next year Parliament
established a Select Committee headed by Sir James
Mackintosh to study the death penalty. The committee
recommended, and Parliament approved, removal of a
number of crimes from the list of those requiring the
death penalty. Then as now, it seems that the practical—
not the theological or philosophical—arguments against
the death penalty were the most persuasive. The death
penalty had been prescribed as punishment for so many
crimes—over 200, including cutting down a young tree—
that juries were hesitant to convict even in cases of obvious guilt because the punishment did not fit the crime.
This started a long trend toward the abolition of the

death penalty in England. By 1834, the number of capital crimes in the country was reduced to 15, and to four by 1861.

Even before Beccaria started his crusade in Europe, William Penn had had a huge impact on capital punishment in the New World. In the Great Act of 1682, Penn established a precedent for the colony of Pennsylvania, which had a large Quaker population. The death penalty was limited to those convicted of premeditated murder. While he was alive, Penn used his personal power to maintain the law. There was no rise in flagrant crime during the 36 years of the Great Act. Despite this eloquent refutation of the need for capital punishment, upon Penn's death in 1718 England forced on the colony contemporary British law, including all of the capital offenses.

By 1767, Beccaria's writings had been translated into English and were read by British and American intellectuals. In 1777, Thomas Jefferson proposed abolishing capital punishment in Virginia except for cases of murder and treason; in 1785, such a bill was brought before the Virginia legislature, where it was defeated by only one vote.

Shortly after the Revolutionary War ended, the Philadelphia Society for Alleviating the Miseries of Public Prisons was formed. Benjamin Rush, its most outstanding member, wrote a paper in 1787 entitled, "An Enquiry into the Effects of Public Punishments upon Criminals and upon Society." It contained the first reasoned argument in America favoring the abolition of the death penalty. Rush devoted a substantial portion of a second treatise, published in 1792, to a Christian view of the death penalty.

William Bradford, the Pennsylvania (and later U.S.) Attorney General, argued successfully to limit the death penalty to the most severe cases. In 1794, he persuaded the Pennsylvania legislature to limit capital punishment to premeditated murder.

The Philadelphia Society became the center of the prison reform movement throughout the country. The Society was more successful at prison reform than in eliminating capital punishment. In 1808, the Quakers helped establish the first association dedicated to abolishing the death penalty, and in 1845 the American Society for the Abolition of Capital Punishment was organized. Abolition bills were regularly placed before state legislatures in these years. The first great success of this movement occurred in 1847, when Michigan became the first state to outlaw the death penalty altogether. Two others, Rhode Island and Wisconsin, eliminated it prior to the Civil War. Many others greatly reduced the number of capital crimes.

Despite America's flirtation with abolition, slaves and Indians as well as criminals continued to be killed, with or without trial. Public executions still attracted large crowds, such as in 1835 in Maine, when over 10,000 rioted at the state's second enforcement of the death penalty.

36

The growth of the social and psychological sciences following the Civil War emphasized the social dimension of crime and focused on changing society and rehabilitating the criminal instead of punishment and retribution. Zebulon Brockway was a leader in this school of thought and introduced the concept of indeterminant sentencing. A convicted criminal would be given a minimum and a maximum sentence, the exact amount of time served to be determined on the basis of the prisoner's progress in rehabilitation. This way of thinking about punishment was the genesis of our present probation system.

In the late 1800s, Kansas, Iowa, and Colorado experimented with doing away with the death penalty. State legislatures vacillated between reason on one hand and the passions of their constituents on the other. Reason would persuade them to outlaw capital punishment; then a heinous crime would be committed, and then passion would drive public debate and the death penalty would be reinstated. This pattern characterized more than a century of struggle over this issue.

After World War I, the abolitionist cause saw the rise of one of its most eloquent spokespersons, Unitarian-turned-agnostic lawyer Clarence Darrow. Champion of despised people and unpopular causes, Darrow found both themes coming together in his work as a defense attorney and an advocate for the abolition of the death penalty. His 1924 defense of Richard Loeb and Nathan Leopold, who had confessed to the murder of a young boy, led to their receiving life imprisonment rather than death.

Carrying the social sciences and scientific penology to the extreme, Darrow believed in social determinism; i.e., no individual moral responsibility. Humans turned to crime because society made them that way, not because of their own free will, Darrow taught. He believed correctional institutions should be modeled along the lines of hospitals and schools rather than traditional jails or prisons. While most people rejected his views, Darrow influenced later liberal Protestant and even Roman Catholic thinking with respect to the role of society in shaping personalities.

The Leopold and Loeb case seemed to revitalize the flagging abolitionist movement. In 1925, the League for the Abolition of Capital Punishment was formed in New York, and in February 1926 it launched its national campaign in New York City just 24 hours before Darrow addressed Congress on the issue. The efforts of the league were further spurred by the case of Nicola Sacco and Bartolomeo Vanzetti, who, in spite of considerable evidence of their innocence, were convicted of killing two men during a robbery and sentenced to death. The conviction led to the formation of the Massachusetts Council for the Abolition of the Death Penalty. The wife of Herbert B. Ehrmann, one of the defendants' lawyers, dedicated her life to the overthrow of capital punishment.

Public sentiment continued to seesaw between abolition and retention of the death penalty. A major landmark that emboldened proponents of capital punishment was the kidnapping and subsequent murder of the son of

Charles Lindbergh, the beloved American hero, in New Jersey in 1932. In a case that was shot full of inconsistencies, unprofessional actions by the prosecution and the defense, and media sensationalism, Bruno Richard Hauptmann was convicted of the crime and sentenced to death. (He was electrocuted in 1936.) In response to the public outrage over the crime, the federal government passed what was popularly known as the Lindbergh Act, which made kidnapping a federal crime. The act authorized capital punishment if the victim was not liberated unharmed.

Then, in 1948, the case of Caryl Chessman broke onto the public stage. He was found guilty of murder and sentenced to death. Without fame, money, or well-placed friends, Chessman taught himself the law, filing his own appeals. He fought over the next 12 years to prove his innocence and save his life, eventually presenting his case before the U.S. Supreme Court on four different occasions. He wrote four books about his experience, and two films were made about his life.

Increasingly, the public came to see Chessman as a sympathetic figure, and many people felt he was innocent. Chessman's story reignited public debate about capital punishment and brought a few of the mainline religious denominations into the fray. From 1956 through the 1980s, a majority of the Protestant and Roman Catholic religious bodies in the United States and Canada took positions in opposition to capital punishment.

* * *

In 1962, the United Nations issued a report claiming that the revocation of the death penalty has never been shown to result in an increase in crime. Sweden (1972) and Spain (1975) abolished the death penalty; Portugal hasn't had it since 1867. In 1981, France abolished the death penalty, as did several other countries. In 1989, UNESCO ruled that the death penalty should not be used for mentally retarded people. In 1990, the United Nations called on all member nations to take steps toward abolishing capital punishment.

Switzerland outlawed capital punishment in 1992, and our neighbors Canada and Mexico have also abolished the practice. In 1995, South Africa abolished it as well. Why does the United States remain the only developed nation that executes its citizens?

Although we have advanced far beyond the atrocities Damiens experienced in eighteenth-century France, we still hang criminals to death or put them in front of firing squads, and even our allegedly "painless" means of death—electrocution, poison injection, gas—often cause great pain and suffering to the victim. It has been documented that each of these latter methods may bring death only after 15 agonizing minutes. The supposedly humane electric chair, for instance, caused reddish flames to spray from the head of convict Jesse Joseph Tafero in 1990 as his convulsing body slammed up and down against the chair. It was such a lurid display, *Prime Time* host Sam Donaldson declared that death penalty supporters should witness executions like Tafero's so they would understand what they advocate.

In 1924, Leopold and Loeb were given life sentences instead of the death penalty. Loeb died in prison, but Leopold lived for many more years and received parole in 1958, completely rehabilitated after his prison stay. There is a way to deal with perpetrators of heinous crimes, and to fulfill society's need for retribution, without resorting to legalized murder. We do not need the death penalty.

2

ALTERNATIVES TO THE DEATH PENALTY

[T]here is an effective alternative to burning the life out of human beings in the name of public safety. That alternative is just as permanent, at least as great a deterrent and—for those who are so inclined—far less expensive than the exhaustive legal appeals required in capital cases. That alternative is life imprisonment without the possibility of parole.

—Mario Cuomo, Governor of New York, 1989

C an America live without the death penalty? Are there alternatives that would deal with those currently sentenced to death and satisfy the American people?

In the wake of such highly publicized events as the

Oklahoma City bombing and the Simpson murder trial, Americans are increasingly pushing their representatives in government to be tougher on crime. Very often, this pressure is expressed as "Use the death penalty." This sentiment is easily exploited by politicians wishing to burnish their crime-fighting credentials without having to explain the details.

In some states, politicians who favor the death penalty resist stiffer sentences that eliminate parole because they fear that with real alternatives the people will see no more need for the death penalty. Apparently, they would rather have criminals get out of jail sooner than give up the death penalty as a cheap symbol for being tough on crime. In New York, some politicians opposed a life without the possibility of parole bill because its passage would make the death penalty "less of a campaign issue." (See Humbert, "Annual Death Penalty Battle Resumes in NYS," *Cortland Standard*, February 5, 1990.)

In the 1994 New York gubernatorial election, Republican George Pataki made this an issue against Democrat Mario Cuomo, who had used his veto power to keep New York amongst the states that refuse to kill. Pataki won in a close race, and many voters stated that the death penalty issue was a deciding factor for them in supporting Pataki. A year later, with much fanfare, Pataki signed the death penalty into law.

This was not an isolated point in the death penalty debate—for more than 20 years, states have been trying to come up with death penalty statutes that do not contravene the Constitution. The genesis of this phase of the battle was the 1972 Supreme Court decision *Furman v. Georgia*, which briefly eliminated capital punishment in the United States.

In the years preceding *Furman*, the sentencer—either judge or jury—chose between imposing death or a lesser sentence for a person convicted of murder. By allowing judges, and especially juries, the ultimate power to punish a criminal, certain inconsistencies arose, often because of prejudice or sheer whim. Racism, especially in the South, influenced many verdicts. In *Furman*, the Supreme Court called the application of the death penalty cruel and unusual punishment because of its "capriciousness." In his comments on the case, Justice White noted that there was "no meaningful basis for distinguishing the few cases in which [the death penalty] is imposed from the many cases in which it is not."

Every standing death penalty sentence, 558 nationwide, was struck down. But *Furman* did not deem the death penalty itself unconstitutional, only the way it was applied. Thus, the states began to rewrite their capital punishment statutes to include procedural safeguards in sentencing to ensure they would no longer be seen as capricious.

In the 1970s and 1980s, many cases were brought before the courts weighing the constitutionality of the states' remedies. Many of the initial laws were struck down, but with a conservative shift in the Supreme Court and more intensive work by state legislatures, the new laws began to pass muster. More than two-thirds of the states now have the death penalty back on their books.

But reestablishing the death penalty was not the only thing the states did. Beginning in a few progressive strongholds and eventually spreading to a majority of the states, the legislatures added an alternative to capital punishment that would keep society safe without needlessly taking human life: life imprisonment without the possibility of parole.

This alternative arose out of the concerns that many citizens and legislators have over the effectiveness of the death penalty as a deterrent and as a fair means of punishment. When I speak to citizens, I find that there are many issues that raise doubts in their minds about capital punishment. Racism is one, especially because of the Rodney King beating and subsequent high-profile cases. These cases symbolize for many Americans the perception of racial injustice within the criminal justice system.

Americans also express great concern over the possibility that an innocent person may be killed by the state for a crime he or she did not commit. In the book *In Spite of Innocence*, authors Radelet, Bedau, and Putnam discuss over 400 cases in which the defendant was wrongly convicted of a crime punishable by death. At least 23 cases have resulted in the execution of innocent people. In fact, when the Supreme Court commuted all death sentences in 1972, five of those who were on death row at the time went on to prove their innocence. Without

45

the good fortune of a major Supreme Court decision, their lives may well have been sacrificed. As the number of death row inmates across the country—now more than 3,000—continues to set new records, the pace of executions accelerates, and the safeguard of *habeas corpus* is reduced, the probability of more innocent people receiving the death penalty increases. This will likely increase the doubts Americans have about the ultimate punishment.

Another factor in the decision to add life without parole as another option in capital sentencing was the public's perception of "revolving-door prisons," which crystallized nationally in George Bush's use of the Willie Horton case in Massachusetts to defeat Michael Dukakis in the 1988 presidential race. The fear that the justice system will parole a murderer capable of repeating a horrendous act motivated officials in many states to come up with a tougher punishment than the existing life sentences.

Life without parole also alleviates the burden of appeals in capital cases. Since *Furman*, the ratio of death sentences handed down to the number of people actually executed is twenty to one. Given appeals, commutations, and death from other causes, the chance that any individual on death row will be executed is quite low. The public often sees the lengthy appeals process as one of the problems with the criminal justice system—thus the current rush to limit appeals in capital cases. But because of the terminal nature of the death penalty, an exhaustive appeals process must exist. Life without the possibility of parole is not as final as the death penalty, and so the need for costly appeals is lessened.

Life without the possibility of parole is also more cost-efficient than the death penalty. It costs states roughly $25,000 a year to house a defendant on death row. If the convict were sentenced at age 25 and died at age 65—40 years in jail—the state will have spent a total of $1 million on him. However, the death penalty itself, with all its appeals, can cost a state anywhere from $2 million to $4 million. The amount saved adds up, especially in California where there are over 250 capital cases a year. Appeals can go on for almost a decade, and 40 percent of death sentences are eventually overturned. In Alabama, the price of one death penalty case could cover prison costs for almost seven convicts for 40 years.

Eugene Wanger, a Michigan attorney greatly responsible for getting the state to include its ban on capital punishment in its constitution (the Michigan legislature banned capital punishment in 1847), claims that the abolition of the death penalty has saved Michigan millions of dollars. "The death penalty system is staggeringly expensive, both in litigation and prison costs," he says. "We've been able to devote more of our resources to finding effective ways to fight and prevent crime instead of lulling the public into a false sense of security with the death penalty." Instead of attacking crime after it is committed, states which have eliminated capital punishment free up the funds to preclude crime through proven programs like gun control, drug rehabilitation, employment opportunities, and early intervention for abused and mentally handicapped children. (See Katz, "The Death Penalty: Yea or Nay," *Newsday*, June 20, 1989.)

Some argue that even if money is saved by life without the possibility of parole, the cost of an aging prison population will be high. Obviously, as a defendant convicted of murder reaches his 60s and 70s he will be susceptible to more medical problems. Many states have taken this into account, providing an alternative of life without the possibility of parole for 25 years. Studies show that criminals are at their most violent at age 18; a convict released at age 55 or 60 poses a substantially lesser threat to society.

The idea of life without parole is as old as the Tower of London, but it has been slow to gain popularity in the United States. In large part, this is due to the attitude instilled by the nineteenth-century prison reform movement: that prison is a means of rehabilitation. Another stumbling block is the public misconception that such a policy causes overcrowded jails. Quietly, though, legislators have been increasing the applicability of this sort of sentence. While some states have rather limited sentencing structures, others have chosen different approaches.

Although no two states share the exact same capital sentencing format, those that have the life without parole alternative can be divided into discrete categories. The first is the triple-tiered approach employed in five states, including Maryland and Oklahoma. This approach gives sentencers the choice between the death penalty, life without parole, or a regular life sentence. Another triple-tiered approach substitutes life without parole for a minimum number of years (usually at least 20) for life without parole. After the minimum period expires, the opportunity for parole returns, but this guaranteed amount of time is usually much longer than a typical life sentence. (The concept underlying the idea is to remove the convicted murderer from society between the ages of 20 and 45, when experience shows he is most likely to commit any type of violent crime.)

In conjunction with life without the possibility of parole, many Americans favor restitution for capital crimes. This would require the convicted murderer to work during the prison term to pay back, in some sense, the victim's family. For instance, if a prisoner worked 40 hours a week, 50 weeks per year, over 25 years at $3 an hour, that would mean $150,000 in restitution. (See Bowers and Vandiver, "People Want an Alternative to the Death Penalty," January 15, 1993.)

Second, some states have a double-tiered system for the most violent crimes. The sentencer must choose between the death penalty or some form of life without parole.

Third, 12 states do not have the death penalty in any form. These states may have only a regular life system, in which the inmate may apply for parole after serving a certain percentage of their "life" term. They may also offer a stricter approach which allows a choice between life without parole and a regular life sentence. A few states even have a single-tiered system in which a defendant convicted of murder in a capital trial is automatically sentenced to life in prison without parole, no matter the circumstances.

A total of 33 states, plus the District of Columbia and the federal government, have within their sentencing statutes some form of life without parole. A total of 14 states have the option of a life sentence in which parole is not possible for 25 years. Even in those few states where parole is possible in less than 25 years, it is very unlikely that those convicted of the worst crimes would be paroled on their first try, if ever. In addition, at least 14 states have a form of life without parole for serious repeat offenders, drug traffickers, and kingpins. This alternative accomplishes the same goal as does the death penalty; it removes convicted murderers from society forever, or at least during the years when they would pose a threat to others.

Despite the availability of this type of sentencing, the majority of Americans continue to believe that even those sentenced to life without parole will eventually be set free. Such notorious criminals as Charles Manson and Sirhan Sirhan were sentenced under milder pre-Furman laws, which allowed for appeal for release on parole. Each time these criminals come up for parole, the media mill gives us retrospectives about their crimes, and the drums for the death penalty beats louder.

For defendants sentenced today, however, the prospects are quite different. The perception that a murderer convicted of a capital crime will be back on the streets in a few years is simply inaccurate. And apart from a commutation or overturned convictions of crimes committed by someone else, prisoners who are locked up for life under this system remain in jail for life. They age and eventually die behind bars, with no chance of returning to society. In California, which is seen as more liberal on capital punishment than states like Florida or Texas, no prisoner sentenced to life without parole has left the state's prison system in the past 25 years.

Two case studies demonstrate the effectiveness of life without parole as a meaningful, practical alternative to the death penalty.

In Alabama, life without the possibility of parole has been met with praise, where it is seen not only as an alternative to the death penalty, but as a more efficient means of sentencing. Prosecutors welcome another choice when trying capital cases because of the public's perception of the regular life sentence as too lenient. Having this extra weapon means prosecutors do not have to pursue the death penalty as the only alternative to letting a convicted murderer walk free.

And the Alabama experience has shown that an increase in those sentenced to serve life without parole does not lead directly to overcrowded prisons. The proportion of all Alabama prisoners who are truly incarcerated for life is less than 9 percent, not even close to being a major reason for overcrowding. We should look to how we handle other types of criminals for relief for our bursting prisons. More than 900,000 arrests are made each year in the United States for drug abuse violations, and more than 1 million for larceny. By contrast, less than 20,000 are arrested for murder each year.

Alabama has also had a generally positive experience with the behavior of the prison "lifers." A general perception is that lifetime inmates will become extremely violent, for what have they got to lose? Many prison officials in other states argue that while short-term prisoners may be coerced into cooperating by promises of parole for good behavior, those spending the rest of their lives in prison cannot be controlled by such incentives. However, as Alabama has learned, there are other means of rewarding or punishing inmates in prison for life: by restricting or expanding prison privileges, or by using in-house punishments like solitary confinement. For someone who is in prison for life, these privileges are important for day-to-day living. In fact, a study of the Alabama prison system reveals that prisoners sentenced to life without the possibility of parole "commit 50 percent fewer disciplinary offenses per capita than all others combined."

This revelation is confirmed in other states. In Michigan, "lifers" have proved to be some of the most disciplined prisoners. They become institutionalized over a period of time, adopting the prison structure as home, since they have no alternative. To fight the system for 25 or more years, they realize, is useless. Leo Lalonde, a Michigan Department of Corrections official, observes that "After a few years, lifers become your better prisoners. They tend to adjust and just do their time. They tend to be a calming influence on the younger kids, and we have more problems with people serving short terms." (See Katz, *Newsday*.)

While Alabama offers only two choices in the most serious capital cases, Kentucky's justice system is notable for the flexibility it gives to prosecutors, defenders, and those handing down sentences. In 1986, the Kentucky legislature passed the Truth in Sentencing Act in order to lengthen the time violent offenders—especially murderers—spend behind bars. They added to the existing statutes the option of a minimum term of 25 years without parole, which sentence would run longer than the standard life sentence. This is tougher than a regular life sentence, but does not carry the finality of capital punishment.

Kentucky's prosecutors now have a whole range of sentences to pursue, allowing them to truly make the punishment fit the crime. Besides the death penalty, they can choose life without the possibility of parole, life without the possibility of parole for 25 years, or a regular life sentence. Juries and judges also can tailor their sentences more accurately to the individual crime. The system is also popular with the state's citizens, who sought tougher sentencing.

Despite the obvious advantages that life without parole has over the death penalty, 75 to 80 percent of the American public in recent polls appears to support capital punishment. How can this be?

First, crime—especially shocking, violent, murderous crime—is an emotional issue. Every day in our country we are faced with heinous, inhuman acts, and we feel powerless to stop them. "Kill them!" seems to be the quick and easy answer.

Second, alternatives to the death penalty are sometimes difficult to explain. Most people are unprepared to discuss the technicalities of criminal sentencing.

Third, it is easier for politicians and other orators to shout "Death penalty!" than it is for them to shout "Life in prison without the possibility of parole!"

And fourth, the public still doesn't believe—and few government officials are telling them—that the criminal justice system will keep violent criminals out of society for more than a few years.

However, once people are told the truth about tough alternative sentences in a clear, cogent fashion, support for the death penalty drops precipitously. A 1993 national survey by Greenberg/Lake and the Tarrance Group showed that, when the sentence of life without the possibility of parole coupled with restitution is offered as an alternative, only 41 percent of respondents supported capital punishment, with 44 percent choosing life without the possibility of parole. Even the choice of a sentence which guaranteed restitution and no release for at least 25 years caused death penalty support to drop by 33 percent. A Gallup poll similarly showed that nationwide support for the death penalty dropped 20 percent when respondents were told about the option of life without the possibility of parole. (See Zeisel and Gallup, "Death Penalty Sentiment in the United States," *Journal of Quantitative Criminology* 5:290, 1989.) These statistics have been reinforced by similar results in various state polls, including those conducted in notorious death penalty states like Georgia and Florida.

In some states which offer only a choice between the death penalty or a regular life sentence, juries are very often unsettled with the limits on sentencing. Georgia, for example, recently included the option of life without parole to the death penalty and life with the possibility of parole. Before life without parole was added, jurors often found themselves in the unsavory position of recommending that a human being be put to death or hoping that a convicted murderer would not strike again when released into society. This Hobson's choice—taking human life or protecting the public—obviously weighed heavily on the jurors (and by extension, the public), for Georgia juries consistently asked the judge if the defendant would be released on parole if a life sentence were handed down.

Yet, though a convicted murderer in Georgia averages 25 years in jail, the law prohibits judges or other legal administrators to give juries any information about the eventual eligibility of the defendant being sentenced. As in most states with capital punishment, Georgia juries had to make their decisions bereft of any knowledge of alternatives to the death penalty. They could not tell whether or not a person who was convicted of aggravated murder would soon be walking the streets with them again. Given such a frightening (although unfounded) prospect, juries frequently chose the death penalty because it represented the only choice assuring complete safety.

Take, for instance, the 1985 Georgia case of James Randall Rogers, in which the jury questioned the judge about the possibility of parole. The judge was forced to insist to the jury that they were not to bring parole into their consideration in their decision. Thirty-four minutes later the jury returned with a death sentence. When polled, 10 of the 12 jurors said that the parole question was indeed a factor in their sentencing, and many said that it was the primary one. One juror was quoted as saying, "We really felt like we didn't have any alternative."

So it goes with most people, who unfortunately believe that the only choice is between death or releasing the prisoner early. As the late Georgia Supreme Court Judge Charles Weltner said, "Everybody believes that a person sentenced to life for murder will be walking the streets within seven years." With an added option of life without parole or life without parole for 25 years, Weltner agreed that the number of death penalties handed down would fall. But information about such options must be available and clear to the sentencing jury. Otherwise a jury's decision will be based on speculation at best and wrong information at worst, making the sentencing procedure capricious and therefore in violation of the *Furman* decision.

It is obvious then that if Americans became generally

aware of life without the possibility of parole as a viable means of punishing violent criminals, the death penalty would not be featured so prominently in our national discourse. We simply have too many doubts about capital punishment.

Finally, what about the family and loved ones of the victim? What serves them best? The death penalty serves the purpose of revenge, which some say is the best form of retribution. Yet the argument that capital punishment eases the grief of a victim's family is questionable, especially in a nation where there are only 25 executions for 25,000 murders each year. As many family members attest, neither the death penalty nor its alternatives can substitute for the tremendous loss of a loved one. However, the threat of an execution means that there will almost always be a lengthy trial and years of appeals. Marietta Jaeger, whose seven-year-old daughter Susie was kidnapped and murdered, never felt the death penalty offered any solace. In a letter to the Death Penalty Information Center, she wrote: "The death penalty causes family members more pain than other sentences. The continuous sequence of courtroom scenes inherent in death penalty cases only serve to keep emotional wounds raw and in pain for years." Many relatives of victims also believe that the death penalty will inflict the same pain they have felt on the accused's family. There is no need, they say, to pursue even more killing.

57

America may now be ready to abandon the death penalty. People strongly prefer alternative sentences to the death penalty once they are given the choice. They want to be sure that murderers will not be released after a few years and that the families of victims will be compensated for their tragedy. The lengthy sentences which people prefer and which guarantee that convicted murderers will stay behind bars are now in place in almost every state in the country. To the extent that support for the death penalty continues, it is because the public in general, and jurors in capital cases in particular, are still unaware of this fundamental change in U.S. sentencing practice.

3

INNOCENCE AND THE DEATH PENALTY
THE DANGER OF MISTAKEN EXECUTIONS

It is better to risk saving a guilty person than to condemn an innocent one.

—Voltaire

Texas is a killer of a state. One hundred and four inmates have been put to death in the Longhorn State since executions resumed there in 1982. Eighteen executions were scheduled for the first half of 1995. And the pace will pick up, for Governor George Bush has signed into law a new "speedy death" bill, which he had made a cornerstone of his election campaign. The average inmate's residency on death row in Texas is now eight years. The law supported by Governor Bush and his attorney general, Dan Morales, short-circuits the appeals process and cuts this wait in half.

Justice delayed may be justice denied, but the speedy execution of an innocent man can only be called murder.

SINCE YOU'RE THE NIGGER, YOU'RE ELECTED

Sometimes racial prejudice, combined with being in the wrong place at the wrong time, propels an innocent person into the role of despicable death row inmate. On Saturday morning, August 23, 1980, a yellow school bus bearing the Bellville, Texas girl's volleyball squad pulled up to Conroe High School, 40 miles north of Houston. The school was relatively empty that day, for the school year hadn't started yet. The team's manager, Cheryl Dee Ferguson, was a vibrant, well-liked 16-year-old known as "Fergy" who was about to begin her junior year and was active in many afterschool activities. She was one of the most popular girls at school, 5'7" tall, with long blond hair, hazel eyes, and an attractive smile.

Soon after getting off the bus, Cheryl went to the girl's washroom and never returned. During the team's warm-up, her coach realized her absence and sent two players to look for her. They returned empty-handed. The coach had the entire team split up to carefully search the school for Fergy, but no one could find her. Despite their fear and concern, the team played its match.

After the match, Cheryl still had not shown up and

an intensive, frantic search began. Two hours later, two janitors found Cheryl's naked body in a dusty loft above the school's auditorium. The janitors were Henry "Icky" Peace and his supervisor, Clarence Brandley, and they immediately became prime suspects. They were questioned, fingerprinted, and asked for hair and blood samples. They both cooperated fully. In order to demonstrate his innocence, Brandley, then 28, voluntarily gave the police samples of his hair and clothing and submitted to a lie detector test, which he passed. But then a frightening thing happened. The police officer interviewing the two janitors told them, "One of the two of you is going to hang for this." Turning to Brandley, the officer added, "Since you're the nigger, you're elected."

The autopsy revealed that Ferguson had been strangled and raped and that she may have already been dead when she was molested. The bruises on her arms indicated that she had been held down with great force. On her skin was a permanent indentation of the crucifix she had been wearing, attesting to the brutality of the attack.

Conroe was in a state of shock. Parents threatened to keep their daughters home from school until the murderer was caught. Texas Ranger Wesley Styles abandoned his vacation to head the probe in Conroe. By the time he arrived in Conroe it was already August 29, nearly a week after the deadly attack. Because school was scheduled to start the following Monday, Styles needed immediate results. Only a few hours after he took over the investigation, Styles arrested Brandley for the murder. Although

61

Conroe High had three other janitors, Brandley was the only black man.

Conroe had both African American and white residents, but they were largely segregated. An old railroad town, Conroe's minority population literally lived on the wrong side of the tracks. The Ku Klux Klan remained active in this East Texas area, where racism has deep roots.

Mike DeGeurin, the fearless defense counsel who represented Brandley during his appeal in 1983, recalled, "People were afraid to send their kids to school until someone was caught. They began with a blind focus on Clarence Brandley, and any circumstance that was inconsistent with that was destroyed or discounted."

From the very beginning, Brandley firmly insisted that he was innocent. The prosecution's case was based solely on weak circumstantial evidence, with no blood, DNA, hair, or fingerprint evidence. Even so, Brandley's trial ended in a hung jury: eleven to one in favor of conviction. The one dissenting member of the all-white jury was William Srack, who almost became a hung juror. Srack says that the other jurors called him "nigger-lover" during deliberations. After the trial Srack was harassed with telephone calls threatening to get him for saving the "nigger."

The prosecution tried again. At the second trial, in February 1982, again before an all-white jury, Brandley was convicted of murder. The prosecutor had again used his peremptory strikes to eliminate all blacks from the jury pool. On Valentine's Day—the day after the jury

announced its verdict, Judge Martin followed the jury's recommendation and sentenced Brandley to death.

Eleven months after the conviction, while Brandley's attorneys were preparing an appeal, they learned that 166 of the 309 exhibits used at trial, many of which offered grounds for appeal, had vanished. Among the missing exhibits was a sperm sample from the victim that could have proved Brandley's innocence with newly developed DNA testing methods. Also missing were hair samples found near the victim's vagina and on her socks. Three of these hairs were reddish blond, matching neither Brandley's nor Ferguson's. These too could have pointed to the real rapist.

In May 1985, three years after Brandley's conviction, the Texas Court of Criminal Appeals affirmed the conviction and death sentence. A few months later Brandley was given his execution date: January 16, 1986. For Brandley, the realization was like hitting a brick wall: he was going to die by lethal injection in Huntsville, the Mecca of the death penalty in Texas.

Brandley's attorneys filed a separate lawsuit known as a *habeas corpus* proceeding, seeking his freedom because the state had lost or destroyed crucial evidence that could have led to a dismissal of the charges. (This is the legal procedure that many of our representatives in Congress are trying to cut off.) Because of the substantial amount of the missing evidence, the court issued an order granting a hearing and postponed the looming execution date.

At that same time, Brandley got his first real break.

Brenda Medina, a woman from nearby Cut 'n' Shoot, Texas, came forward with possible evidence of Brandley's innocence. A former boyfriend, James Dexter Robinson, had confessed to her that he had raped and murdered a young girl about the time that Cheryl Ferguson was victimized. Robinson had been a janitor at Conroe High, but had been fired about a month before the incident. After the rape-murder, Robinson fled to South Carolina, he told her, because he had "killed a girl" and had hidden the body, leaving behind a pair of blood-stained sneakers.

When Medina learned that Brandley had been convicted of Ferguson's murder, she met with an attorney who directed her to tell her story to the district attorney. However, the district attorney did not believe Medina's story, and he did not tell Brandley's attorney about it. Luckily, the first attorney that Medina had consulted informed Brandley's counsel of the stunning confession.

In 1987, after six years of fruitless appeals and massive civil rights demonstrations in support of Brandley, the Texas Court of Criminal Appeals ordered an evidentiary hearing to investigate all the allegations that had come to light. Judge Perry Pickett, presiding, wrote a stinging condemnation of the procedures the prosecution used in Brandley's case, and stated, "The court unequivocally concludes that the color of Clarence Brandley's skin was a substantial factor which pervaded all aspects of the State's capital prosecution of him."

Despite this finding, in late February 1987, Brandley was given a new execution date—March 26, 1987—

barely a month away. A thousand citizens marched through the streets of Conroe protesting the scheduled execution. Amnesty International joined the protest and demanded a meeting with the governor. As the shadow of death approached, Brandley wrote his last will and testament, neatly packed his books and his belongings, and moved to the execution cell to begin his final goodbyes. Eventually, the attorney general joined the cry for a delay of the execution order to allow Brandley's attorneys time to gather newly discovered evidence. A delay was granted, providing Brandley with precious breathing room.

In 1989, after a flurry of publicity that included a *Sixty Minutes* segment and a *700 Club* piece, the Texas Court of Criminal Appeals reversed Brandley's conviction by a vote of six to three. Relying on the 1987 evidentiary hearing in which Judge Pickett found that the prosecutors had railroaded Brandley out of racially based motives, the appellate court ordered a new trial where Brandley would be allowed to present new evidence of his innocence. But he did not have to go through it one more time, for prosecutors decided to drop the charges because they felt they would lose a third trial.

Finally, in 1990, after spending nearly a decade on death row, Brandley was freed. He was then 38. Brandley, charged with murder at age 28, was a free man at age 38. He has gone forward from that point, but he can never get back his missing decade.

Under the new, streamlined Texas law, Brandley would almost surely have been executed.

OUT OF THE SPOTLIGHT'S GLARE

We only know about the injustice to Clarence Brandley because he was in the bright spotlight of the news media, the favored subject of a *Sixty Minutes* profile. It took many years and a tremendous effort by outside counsel, civil rights organizers, special investigators, and the media to save Brandley's life. For others on death row, it is nearly impossible to get even a hearing on a claim of innocence. The fact that Brandley's life was saved does not show that the system works: it merely demonstrates that mistakes happen and that with extraordinary efforts mistakes are sometimes corrected.

But what about defendants who do not become a cause célèbre? We cannot rely on the media to correct every injustice that occurs in our legal system. We must have other safeguards. What review system do we have when a defendant is sentenced to death, and newly discovered evidence suggests that the accused is in fact innocent? There is no time limit on the truth.

Brandley remembers his first days of freedom, when his sister cooked him his favorite meal and his mother's smile returned to her face. Now 44 and the pastor of a small church in Houston called God's House, he truly savors freedom now and spends his time working to get other innocents released from death row. In this work, Brandley is fighting a rising tide of death. From New York to Texas and in the halls of Congress, a popular movement is growing to limit appeals and be done with those on death row. Although he is a living, breathing example of an innocent person wrongfully accused, incarcerated, and almost executed, our leaders don't seem to care. Most Republicans and many Democrats are saying, "Cut the budget—chop their heads off."

This rush to "justice" would have killed Clarence Brandley and others who have been wrongly convicted and sentenced to die. Jim McCloskey, head of Centurion Ministries, a Princeton, New Jersey agency that works on behalf of the wrongly convicted, has succeeded in freeing at least 15 innocents from jail. "There are a lot of common characteristics that combine to create false convictions—prosecutorial and police [misconduct], lazy investigators, and poor defense lawyering," McCloskey says.

THE CASE OF RANDALL ADAMS

Texas maintains a Wild West attitude, a gunslinging mentality, that killers should be hunted down and that the death penalty should be imposed. This principle especially applies to the killers of policemen.

On November 28, 1976, Dallas police officer Robert Wood, a full-blooded Choctaw Indian, was shot to death while stopping a dirty blue car to warn the driver he was driving without headlights on. Dallas has a proud history of apprehending copkillers within 24 hours. The killer of Robert Wood was not arrested within the first few days after the killing and the pressure to find a suspect was growing intense.

67

The police interrogated 16-year-old David Harris, who admitted stealing a blue Mercury Comet and further admitted that it was this car that was pulled over by Officer Wood on the fateful November day. Harris convinced the police that Randall Adams, a white man, was the actual murderer and that he would testify against Adams. Harris had met Adams at a gas station, and the two had gone to a movie together.

The problem with Harris's story was that Adams was not with Harris when Wood was gunned down. Nevertheless, the Dallas police tried to make Adams sign a confession. He absolutely refused, claiming all the while that he was innocent. They tried to make him pick up the murder weapon. When they failed, Sergeant Gus Rose pulled his own gun, cocked it, and pointed it at Adams's head. Rose said, "I ought to blow your shit away."

Primarily on the basis of Harris's testimony, a jury convicted Adams of murder and sentenced him to death. His attorneys appealed all the way to the highest court in Texas, but were rejected. After those appeals failed, Adams was called back to court and given the date for his execution: May 8, 1979. His attorneys filed an immediate request to the U.S. Supreme Court for a stay of execution.

Adams was not hopeful. While on death row, he counted the days to his imminent death. May 8 came and went, and Adams heard nothing from the warden or the courts. He kept his silence, thankful to have the opportunity to draw these extra breaths of life. At least he had not yet not been taken to Huntsville.

Two days after he was scheduled to die, he received a letter from his attorney advising him that the Supreme Court had postponed his execution until it had an opportunity to review his case. Adams recalled, "Slowly I began to climb out of the pit that was meant to be my grave. My eyes were opened to life in a new way. I was sure that there was some reason for all of this."

Texas has a long and proud tradition of hanging judges and hanging juries. In fact, the Texas Penal Code insists that jurors are to be excused from duty if they are opposed to the death penalty in whole or in part. It was this issue that grabbed the attention of the Supreme Court, which takes only a few cases out of every hundred submitted for review. Some aspect of the case must include a serious constitutional infirmity for the court even to consider a hearing. In Adams's case, several jurors had been excluded from the jury because they could not swear that the mandatory death penalty would not affect their decision. Jurors were required to impose a sentence of death if they found that the killer was likely to be dangerous in the future.

On March 24, 1980, Adams's case was argued before the Supreme Court. Adams, of course, did not get to see or hear the arguments, for he remained confined to the cold, tomblike Texas death row. He knew that his case was argued before the highest court in the land, and he became somewhat of a local hero because of the distinction.

Three long months later, Adams heard the decision in a most offhand way—a guard stopped by his cell to say that he had just heard a Huntsville radio station announce that Adams had won his case. The Supreme Court had overturned his conviction by an eight-to-one vote, with Justice William Rehnquist the sole dissenting vote.

But Adams's happiness was short-lived. Governor Bill Clements, in an attempt to sidestep the Supreme Court's ruling, commuted the sentence to life imprisonment. Adams remained an involuntary ward of the Texas Department of Corrections.

Eight hard years later, Errol Morris released his documentary film *The Thin Blue Line*, which described Adams's case and led to a public outcry for his release. *The Reporters*, a Fox television program, broadcast an interview with David Harris, who finally admitted that he had indeed killed Officer Wood and that Adams was not with him at the time of the slaying. Because of this videotaped confession, Texas finally agreed to release Randall Adams.

No facet of the debate about capital punishment is more disturbing to me than the prospect that the government executes innocent people. Because the absolute number of death sentences is increasing rapidly, and because appeals of these capital cases are being severely limited, we are going to see the death of scores, and possibly hundreds, of innocent defendants. Even William Rehnquist, now Chief Justice of the Supreme Court and a true fan of capital punishment, strongly implied that innocent men and women will be convicted: "It is an unalterable fact that our judicial system, like the human beings who administer it, is fallible," Rehnquist noted while approving the execution of Leonel Herrera, despite strong evidence that Herrera was wrongly convicted and sentenced to death.

A recent national poll found that the number one issue raising doubts among voters regarding the death penalty is the danger of mistaken executions. Fifty-eight percent of voters are disturbed that the death penalty might allow an innocent person to be killed by a lethal injection, literally fired to death in an electric chair, or asphyxiated by poisonous gas.

HOW MANY INNOCENTS?

The most conclusive evidence that scores of innocent people may be languishing on death row comes from the surprisingly large number of death row inmates whose convictions have been overturned by the courts. Professors Michael Radelet and Hugo Bedau have spent 30 years researching Americans wrongly convicted of capital offenses. They have documented 400 cases of innocents convicted of rape, murder, and other serious offenses subject to a possible death sentence.

Since 1970, at least 59 prisoners have been released from death row based on evidence of their innocence. Some of these men (and nearly all of those on death row are males) were convicted on the basis of perjured testimony or because the prosecutor improperly withheld exculpatory evidence. In some cases a biased judge or jury ruled against a defendant whose sole crime was being in the wrong place at the wrong time. In other cases, the true killer was caught and admitted to the crime. God is omniscient, but human beings are not. When we try to play God, tragedy is the inevitable result. Removal from society for life, not removal from God's world, ought to be enough to protect society from those who endanger it and from those who threaten the lives of their fellow human beings.

For every death sentence that is reversed because of a wrongful conviction, there are more innocent inmates who remain on death row waiting to be executed. In England, the case of Timothy Evans, who was pardoned ten years after he was hung, played a significant role in that country's decision to abolish the death penalty. England also recently officially acknowledged that Derek Bentley, a mentally disabled teenager executed for killing a police officer just prior to the abolition of the death penalty, should not have been hanged for the crime. There has been no such conclusion in the case of Ricky Ray Rector, the lobotomized man then-Arkansas governor Bill Clinton put to death in the middle of his 1992 presidential campaign to prove his toughness on crime and to divert attention from the Gennifer Flowers affair, which was interfering with the New Hampshire primary. (See Marshall Frahey, *The New Yorker*, 1994.)

Roy Jenkins, former British Home Secretary and the cabinet minister who was responsible for commuting death sentences, remarked, "It is my view that the frailty of human judgment . . . is too great to support the finality of capital punishment."

A series of recent cases in this country in which innocent men have been released after serving years on death row has increased public awareness of this issue. Hearings have been held recently before both Senate and House committees regarding what should be done to prevent future injustices.

INNOCENCE IS NOT GENERALLY REVIEWED

Whatever the cause, erroneous convictions are most damaging in death penalty cases because the sentence may be carried out before the innocent person has a chance to disprove his or her guilt. As the final date comes closer, the legal system becomes locked in a battle over procedural issues rather than in a search for the truth. In most states there simply is no formal procedure for hearing new evidence of a defendant's innocence prior to his execution. Thus, accounts reporting that a particular case has been appealed numerous times before many judges may be misleading. Most often, the defendant's innocence is not being argued and reviewed by these tribunals; only the death penalty procedures are being discussed.

For example, when Roger Keith Coleman was

73

executed in Virginia in 1992, it was reported that his last appeal to the Supreme Court was Coleman's sixteenth round in court. However, the Supreme Court had earlier declared that Coleman's constitutional claims were barred from any review in federal court because his prior attorneys had filed an appeal too late in 1986. His evidence was similarly excluded from review in state court as well. Coleman's innocence was debated only in the news media, and considerable doubt concerning his guilt went with him to his execution.

WHERE DOES THE SYSTEM BREAK DOWN?

A brief description of some of the recent cases in which death row inmates have been exonerated helps illustrate how these mistakes are made.

Official Misconduct: James Richardson

In the case of James Richardson in Florida, years of work by volunteer attorneys led Janet Reno and the Miami prosecutor's office to conduct an investigation resulting in a finding of innocence. Richardson was convicted of poisoning his own children and sentenced to death in 1968. The threat of execution was removed when the Supreme Court overturned all existing death sentences in 1972. Seventeen years later, Reno, then Dade County State's Attorney, was appointed special investigator in Richardson's case and concluded that the state had "knowingly used perjured testimony and suppressed evidence helpful to the defense." Richardson was freed 21 years after being sentenced to death and long after he would have been executed, but for the Supreme Court's intervention in other cases.

It is an inescapable fact of our criminal justice system that innocent people are sometimes convicted of crimes. In the course of a defendant's appeals, or sometimes only many years later, new evidence will emerge which clearly demonstrates that the wrong person was prosecuted and convicted of a crime.

The Pressure to Prosecute: Walter McMillian

In 1986, in the small town of Monroeville, Alabama, an 18-year-old white woman was shot to death in a dry cleaner's shop around 10 A.M. Although the town was shocked by the murder, no one was arrested for eight months. Johnny D. (Walter) McMillian was a black man who lived in the next town. He had been dating a white woman and his son had married a white woman, none of which made Johnny D. popular in Monroeville.

On the day of the murder, Johnny D. was at a fish fry with his friends and relatives. Many of these people gave testimony at trial that Johnny D. could not have committed the murder of Ronda Morrison because he was with them all day. Nevertheless, he was arrested, tried, and convicted of the murder. Indeed, Johnny D. was placed on death row upon his arrest, well before his trial. No physical evidence linked him to the crime, but three people testifying at his trial connected him with the murder. All three witnesses received favors from the state for their incriminating testimony. The same three witnesses later recanted their testimony, including the only "eyewitness," who stated that he was pressured by the prosecutors to implicate Johnny D. in the crime.

The jury in the trial recommended a life sentence for Johnny D., but the judge overruled this recommendation and sentenced him to death. His case went through four rounds of appeal, all of which were denied. New attorneys, not paid by the state of Alabama, voluntarily took over the case and eventually found that the prosecutors had illegally withheld evidence which pointed to McMillian's innocence. A story about the case appeared on *Sixty Minutes* on November 22, 1992. Finally, the state agreed to investigate its earlier handling of the case and then admitted that a grave mistake had been made. McMillian was freed into the welcoming arms of his family and friends on March 3, 1993.

Walter McMillian summed up his feelings: "I was wrenched from my family, from my children, from my grandchildren, from my friends, from my work that I loved, and was placed in an isolation cell the size of a shoebox, with no sunlight, no companionship, and no work for nearly six years. Every minute of every day, I knew I was innocent. . . ."

The Passage of Time: Kirk Bloodsworth

In 1984, Dawn Hamilton, a nine-year-old girl, was brutally raped and murdered in Baltimore County, Maryland. Two young boys and one adult said they had seen Dawn with a man prior to her death. They thought that Kirk Bloodsworth looked like the man who had been with her. No physical evidence linked Bloodsworth to the crime, but he was convicted and sentenced to death because he looked like someone who might have committed the crime.

When a young child is sexually assaulted and murdered, our natural instinct is to seek revenge. All too often that revenge is savaged upon the first person suspected of the crime. That rush to justice, that rush to seek retribution is the human instinct that is very often responsible for killing innocent defendants. I too have great sympathy for innocent rape victims, for innocents harmed by any crime. But it does not help justice to add another innocent victim.

"One of the loneliest feelings I have ever had was when the judge sentenced me to death [and] people in the courtroom started to applaud and stare at me with feelings of glee," Bloodsworth said. "At that point in time I started to realize that this was no longer a dream, but there was a very real possibility that I would be executed, although I was completely innocent."

Some evidence had been gleaned from the crime scene, but it had given the police no clue as to who the killer was. Tests were conducted on the girl's underwear,

77

but the tests were not yet sophisticated enough to detect and identify DNA material from the likely assailant, nor to prove Bloodsworth's innocence. Fortunately for Bloodsworth, he was granted a new trial when a judge ruled that the state had withheld evidence from the defense attorneys about another suspect. This time he received a life sentence. Bloodsworth continued to maintain his innocence, and the life sentence gave him the time to prove it.

When a new volunteer lawyer agreed to look into Bloodsworth's case, he decided to try one more time to have the evidence in the case tested. He sent the underwear to a laboratory in California, which used newly developed DNA techniques. The defense attorney was astonished when he learned that there was testable DNA material. The tests showed that the semen stain on the underwear could not possibly have come from Bloodsworth. The prosecution then agreed that if these results could be duplicated by the FBI's crime laboratory, it would consent to Bloodsworth's release. On June 25, 1993, the FBI's results affirmed what Bloodsworth had been saying all along: he was innocent of all charges. On June 28, he was released by order of the court from the Maryland State Correctional facility in Jessup, after nine brutal years in prison—two of the years on death row.

There are many similar stories of defendants who have spent years on death row, some coming within hours of their execution, only to be released by the courts with all charges dropped. What is noteworthy about the cases described above is that they are very recent examples which illustrate that mistaken death sentences are not a relic of the past. These cases, and the cases of Federico Macias and Gregory Wilhoit, who were released in 1993, and Dennis Williams, released in 1996, point out the inherent fallibility of the criminal justice system. Mistakes and even occasional misconduct are to be expected. But once an execution occurs, there is no redress.

INADEQUACIES IN THE LEGAL SYSTEM

The cases detailed in this chapter might convey a reassuring impression that, although mistakes are made, the appeals system ferrets them out prior to execution. However, what these cases actually illustrate is that the system *sometimes* allows the time for correction of factual errors. These men were found innocent despite the system and only as a result of extraordinary efforts not generally available to death row defendants.

In the case of Walter McMillian, his volunteer outside counsel had obtained from prosecutors an audio-tape of one of the key witnesses' statements incriminating McMillian. After listening to the statement, the attorney flipped the tape over to see if anything was on the other side. It was only then that he heard the same witness complaining that he was being pressured to frame McMillian. With that fortuitous break, the whole case against Johnny D. began to fall apart.

Similarly, proving the innocence of Kirk Bloodsworth

was more a matter of chance than the orderly working of the appeals process. Only a scientific breakthrough allowed Bloodsworth to prove his innocence after years of failed appeals. And even then, the prosecutor was not bound under Maryland law to admit this new evidence.

Furthermore, not every death row inmate is afforded the quality of counsel and resources which McMillian and Bloodsworth were fortunate to have. Many of those on death row go for years without any attorney at all.

One unpredictable element which can affect whether an innocent person is released is the involvement of public opinion and the media. In Randall Adams's case, film producer Errol Morris went to Texas to make a documentary on Dr. James Grigson, the notorious "Dr. Death." Grigson would claim 100 percent certainty for his courtroom predictions that a particular defendant would kill again, and he made such a prediction about Randall Adams.

In the course of his investigation of Grigson, Morris became interested in Adams's plight and helped unearth layers of prosecutorial misconduct in that case. *The Thin Blue Line* told Adams's story in a way no one had seen before. The movie was released in 1988 and Adams was freed the following year.

Similarly, all charges and death sentences against Thomas Gladish, Richard Greer, Ronald Keine, and Clarence Smith were dropped in 1976 thanks, in part, to the *Detroit News* investigation of lies told by the prosecution's star witness. Clarence Brandley's case was aided by the surge of the civil rights community's opposition to his execution: supporters were able to raise $80,000 for his defense, and his story appeared on *Sixty Minutes*. Obviously, these advantages are not available to everyone on death row who may have been wrongly convicted. *Sixty Minutes* could tell the story of a different innocent inmate on death row every week and still not be able to correct every injustice that has condemned a person to wrongful death. While the media does help correct some injustices, we should not have to go outside of the justice system to make our system work.

Another unpredictable element is public opinion. Our system of justice does not make a distinction between defendants who are definitely innocent (i.e., those who are demonstrated to be innocent by some piece of evidence or by another person's confession) and those who are found innocent at trial because of reasonable doubt. The opinion of relatively uninformed people outside the courtroom is not supposed to affect the outcome of a trial, especially when a jury is sequestered. However, a general atmosphere of hatred toward a defendant can penetrate even the best-controlled courtrooms. And certainly judges and attorneys cannot always account for the origins of their own attitudes.

Thus, a judge, a prosecutor, and even a defense attorney may come into a capital trial with preconceived notions about the death penalty and the type of people accused of capital crimes. These notions will absolutely affect the fairness of the trial. And the jurors, although they are conjoined to consider only the facts of the case, bring to their work their own sensibilities, which have been shaped by years of peer pressure, political posturing, and street-corner philosophers. This mixture bodes ill for the chances of a fair, dispassionate capital trial.

Finally, most defendants facing the death penalty cannot afford to hire their own attorneys, and the state is required to provide one, and only one. Not a team of legal heavyweights, not a DNA expert, not a star cross-examiner. Some states have a public defender office staffed by attorneys to handle criminal cases. These public defenders are almost always overworked and underpaid. While they provide the best defense they are able, they often do not have the resources to investigate, to interview, or to even look at all the evidence against their client. Many states do not even have public defender offices. In those states, attorneys are appointed from the local bar, and the quality of this representation is uneven at best.

All death row inmates are assured of representation to make one direct appeal in their state courts. If that appeal is denied, representation is no longer guaranteed. In states like California and Texas, which have large death rows, many defendants sentenced to death are not currently represented by any attorney. Without representation, even if new evidence is discovered, a death row inmate is unlikely to get an appeal heard, much less get a death sentence overturned.

* * *

Supreme Court Justice Thurgood Marshall once said, "No matter how careful courts are, the possibility of perjured testimony, mistaken honest testimony, and human error remain all too real. We have no way of judging how many innocent persons have been executed, but we can be certain that there were some."

I agree with Justice Marshall—we will always have mistakes, human error, and perjury. We will always have rush to justice, hysterical public opinion, and political pressure. As long as we have these problems, innocent people will be convicted and sent to jail. And as long as we have the death penalty, innocent people will die, with no chance of correcting the error.

4

CRUEL AND UNUSUAL PUNISHMENT

IS THE DEATH PENALTY UNCONSTITUTIONAL?

From this day forward, I will no longer tinker with the machinery of death.

—Supreme Court Justice Harry Blackmun

he U.S. Constitution protects the right of American citizens to their life, liberty, and property. In this, it has become the model for other countries wishing to codify human dignity, due process, and fundamental fairness in their own legal standards. The Eighth Amendment in particular—the one prohibiting cruel and unusual punishment—has been duplicated by new nations around the world.

84

Germany and South Africa, two nations born from the ashes of brutal and bloody conflicts, have ruled in favor of life by banning the death penalty in their constitutions. The worldwide trend is toward the abolition of capital punishment. Many so-called "third world" nations have banned capital punishment.

Thus, if the death penalty is the ultimate human rights violation, the United States must be cast into that objectionable status of human rights violator—grouped together with certain other nations who we feel execute people for unjust causes. One of our peers is China, which according to Amnesty International, accounted for 1,419 of a worldwide total of 1,831 executions during 1993.

If the United States is to champion human rights around the world, it must have its own house in order. It is embarrassing to me as I have traveled the globe to expand human rights that on the question of capital punishment the United States is an example of a country where human rights are being lost. We recognize torture as a violation of the Eighth Amendment, but not the ultimate torture—the threat of death and actual execution. Is not death by lethal injection, firing squad, or electric chair cruel and unusual punishment? Is not such punishment just as cruel as stoning or other forms of torture we call primitive? Is it not cruel to keep someone on death row for decades? All of these punishments are exceptionally cruel and barbaric and have no place in modern society. Morally and legally, we are on the wrong side of this issue.

*   *   *

While I am not a lawyer, I certainly understand concepts such as equal protection of the law, and realize that these concepts are as flexible as the justices who interpret them. I remember the great 1954 decision *Brown v. Board of Education*, whereby the Warren Court ruled that separate schools were inherently unequal. This decision overturned *Plessy v. Ferguson* and nearly 60 years of cases that allowed "separate but equal" facilities. Although the U.S. Supreme Court has not yet ruled that the death penalty is unconstitutional because it constitutes cruel and unusual punishment, other American courts have.

I may not be a lawyer, but I know about justice and fairness. I am joined in opposition to the death penalty by legal scholars, prosecutors, and Supreme Court justices. Justice Thurgood Marshall opposed the death penalty on constitutional grounds. Justice Harry Blackmun, appointed to the court by Richard Nixon, at first supported the death penalty and has now come out against it. He believes that the law is evolving toward a civilized justice that will eventually abolish capital punishment.

In 1994 Justice Blackmun wrote the following:

> From this day forward, I will no longer tinker with the machinery of death. For more than 20 years I have endeavored—indeed, I have struggled—along with a majority of this Court, to develop procedural and substantive rules that

would lend more than mere appearance of fairness to the death penalty endeavor. Rather than continue to coddle the Court's delusion that the desired level of fairness has been achieved and the need for regulation eviscerated, I feel morally and intellectually obligated simply to concede that the death penalty experiment has failed.

Blackmun explained that it became evident to him that no combination of rules or regulations could ever save the death penalty from its inherent weaknesses. The basic question he raised was, does the system accurately and consistently determine which defendants "deserve" to die? Firmly and unequivocally, Blackmun answered, "No."

The Supreme Court, Blackmun added, has allowed vague aggravating circumstances to be employed, relevant mitigating circumstances to be disregarded, and vital judicial review to be blocked. The ultimate problem was that factual, legal, and moral error created a system that we know must wrongly kill some defendants, a system that fails to deliver the fair, consistent, and reliable sentences of death required by the Constitution.

In 1972, in *Furman v. Georgia*, the Supreme Court ruled the death penalty was unconstitutional as *administered* because there was no meaningful basis for deciding who lived and who died. The only discernible basis for making that decision, according to Justice Potter Stewart, was that of race, which the Constitution and human decency and fairness does not permit. Justice Blackmun dissented in that case, voting in favor of the death penalty. Now he believes that he was wrong and that Furman was correctly decided. Rarely does a Supreme Court Justice admit his mistakes; it takes great courage and dignity. Blackmun stated:

> There is little doubt that Furman's essential holding was correct. Although most of the public seems to desire, and the Constitution appears to permit, the penalty of death, it surely is beyond dispute that if the death penalty cannot be administered consistently and rationally, it may not be administered at all.

In the years following *Furman*, the states made efforts to comply with its mandate to provide sensible and objective guidelines for determining who should live and who should die. More death penalty cases made their way to the Supreme Court. In 1976 and 1977, the Court heard five cases involving laws passed after *Furman*. It struck down laws in Louisiana and North Carolina, but upheld laws in Georgia, Florida, and Texas.

All the experimentation following the *Furman* case did not improve the administration of the death penalty. Consistency and fairness are usually opposites; that means the facts of each case influence the judge or jury's decision about sentencing. There are myriad mitigating factors, such as a defendant who had never before been violent and is not likely to kill again. How then could laws provide specific guidelines about life and death that would hold across all death penalty cases in a state?

The highest courts in two states recognized this basic flaw in the death penalty. In 1972, the Supreme Court of California ruled that the death penalty was unconstitutional under the state constitution. The California constitution banned "cruel *or* unusual punishment," while the U.S. Constitution bans "cruel *and* unusual punishment." Noting this distinction, the California Supreme Court found the death penalty cruel, and outlawed its use. Later, responding to public pressure, California passed an amendment to its constitution that reinstated the death penalty.

In 1980, the Supreme Court of Massachusetts ruled the death penalty unconstitutional, but for a different reason. After eight years of post-*Furman* experience, the Massachusetts high court realized, as Justice Blackmun would admit 14 years later, that death penalty "reforms" were not working. The court noted, "We think that arbitrariness in sentencing will continue even under the discipline of a post-*Furman* statute" like the one that Massachusetts had passed. The court noted that, "Examination of death penalty sentences imposed in Florida, Georgia and Texas [after *Furman*] . . . indicates that very little has changed as to arbitrariness and discrimination." The court referred to this bone-chilling data: In Florida, 48 percent of the blacks convicted of killing a white person were sentenced to death, while none of 111 whites who were convicted of killing a black person were sentenced to die. Similarly, in Georgia, 37 percent of the African Americans convicted of killing a white person were given death sentences, whereas less than 3 percent (2 of 71) of whites convicted of killing blacks were given the same treatment. Texas painted the same distorted, racist picture: while 27 blacks were sentenced to die for killing whites, of 143 whites who were found to have killed African Americans, none was given the death sentence. The Massachusetts court concluded that the death penalty was primarily reserved for those who kill whites and so ruled the death penalty unconstitutional. The people of Massachusetts have kept this prohibition in force.

At the same time that American state legislatures and courts were going through their contortions over the death penalty, Canada was going through a similar process of public debate and dialogue. The outcome was different north of the border: Canada made its decision to outlaw the death penalty.

In 1977, West Germany's highest court ruled that the death penalty was a violation of that country's constitution: "Respect for human dignity especially requires the prohibition of cruel, inhuman, and degrading punishments. The state cannot turn the offender into an object of crime prevention to the detriment of his constitutionally protected right to social worth and respect." That interpretation now holds for the reunited German nation. And in December of that year, the United Nations General Assembly passed a resolution stating:

> The General Assembly . . . Reaffirms that . . . the main objective to be pursued in the field of capital punishment is that of progressively restricting the number of offenses for which the death penalty may be imposed with a view to the desirability of abolishing this punishment.

It would seem natural for the developed democracies of the world to move away from the death penalty. More telling is that even less-developed countries, which have relatively short experience with representative government and fair justice, are rejecting it as well. Haiti, the scene of three years of brutal killings by General Cédras in the early 1990s and a place where the thirst for revenge might be strong, has abolished the death penalty. And in June 1995, the Constitutional Court of South Africa ruled that the death penalty was unconstitutional.

South Africa's 1993 constitution outlawed "cruel, inhuman or degrading treatment or punishment," a provision that is very similar to our own Eighth Amendment provision against "cruel and unusual punishment." The South African court held:

> Death is the most extreme form of punishment to which a convicted criminal can be subjected. Its

execution is final and irrevocable. It puts an end not only to the right to life itself, but to all other personal rights which had been vested in the deceased under [the constitution]. . . . In the ordinary meaning of the words, the death sentence is undoubtedly a cruel punishment. Once sentenced, the prisoner waits on death row in the company of other prisoners under sentence of death, for the processes of their appeals and the procedures for clemency to be carried out. Throughout this period, those who remain on death row are uncertain of their fate, not knowing whether they will ultimately be reprieved or taken to the gallows. Death is a cruel penalty and the legal processes, which necessarily involve waiting in uncertainty for the sentence to be set aside or carried out, add to the cruelty.

The South African court quoted freely from decisions of the U.S. Supreme Court, as well as from decisions of the California and Massachusetts supreme courts. It stated: "Although the United States Constitution does not contain a specific guarantee of human dignity, it has been accepted by the United States Supreme Court that the concept of human dignity is at the core of the prohibition of 'cruel and unusual punishment' by the Eighth and Fourteenth Amendments."

*, * *

Justice Blackmun asserted that while an innocent person may be sent to prison, sentencing that person to death is intolerable because of the irreversibility of the mistake. He said, "There is a heightened need for fairness in the administration of death. This unique level of fairness is born of the appreciation that death truly is different from all other punishments that a society inflicts upon its citizens." He concluded:

> Perhaps one day this Court will develop procedural rules or verbal formulas that actually will provide consistency, fairness, and reliability in a capital-sentencing scheme. I am not optimistic that such a day will come. I am more optimistic, though, that this Court eventually will conclude that the effort to eliminate arbitrariness while preserving fairness in the infliction of the death penalty is so plainly doomed to failure that it and the death penalty must be abandoned altogether. I may not live to see that day, but I have faith that eventually it will arrive. The path the Court has taken lessens us all.

I am younger than Justice Blackmun and more optimistic that the Supreme Court will come around to his opinion while I am still alive. A few short years ago not many of us would have believed the revolution that took place in South Africa. Nelson Mandela was then in jail and the ruling white elite was seemingly prepared to keep

93

the barricades up forever. Now Nelson Mandela is the duly elected president of South Africa.

We will have the vestiges of the Reagan-Bush era on the Supreme Court for many years to come, but they often represent only a slim majority on the Court. New appointments can tip the balance against capital punishment. Let us appoint in the future enlightened justices who will act, as did the enlightened justices in South Africa, for fairness and against cruelty; for justice and against retribution.

The rulings of the U.S. Supreme Court over the years have shown that the rights protected by the Bill of Rights, like the prohibition against cruel and unusual punishment, are evolving concepts rather than hard and fast rules. More than 200 years ago, the Constitution established that a slave should be counted as only three-fifths of a person for the purposes of the census, and it was generally understood that neither slaves nor women had the right to vote. Despite attempts to hold back the inevitable, we now have a society in which all citizens in good standing have the right to vote.

The same phenomenon is occurring regarding the death penalty. President Clinton, a Democrat, supports the use of the death penalty: the crime bill that he signed into law in 1995 increases the number of capital crimes by 60 at the federal level. This puts him on the same side of the issue as Republican presidents Bush and Reagan. It is the nature of politicians to follow public opinion polls in deciding where they stand on important issues, and as discussed in Chapter 3, the easy answer for the public is to retain the death penalty. Using polls to position oneself in the political center brings short-term electoral gains but long-term societal fallout. We need our nation's leaders to mold public opinion, and to do that they must find the *moral* center, not just the political center. Our leaders, and by extension, our nation, must evolve. We must lead and be a beacon to the world in human rights.

5

DEADLY NUMBERS
RACE, GEOGRAPHY, SEX, AND
THE DEATH PENALTY

*The death penalty symbolizes whom we fear and don't
fear, whom we care about and whose lives are not valid.*
—Bryan Stevenson, director of the
Equal Justice Initiative of Alabama

Who receives the death penalty has less to do
with the violence of the crime than with the
color of the criminal's skin or, more often, the
color of the victim's skin. Murder—always tragic—seems
to be a more heinous and despicable crime in some states
than in others. Women who kill and who are killed are
judged by different standards than are men who are
murderers and victims.

96

The death penalty is essentially an arbitrary punishment. There are no objective rules or guidelines for when a prosecutor should seek the death penalty, when a jury should recommend it, and when a judge should give it. This lack of objective, measurable standards ensures that the application of the death penalty will be discriminatory against racial, gender, and ethnic groups.

The majority of Americans who support the death penalty believe, or wish to believe, that legitimate factors such as the violence and cruelty with which the crime was committed, a defendant's culpability or history of violence, and the number of victims involved determine who is sentenced to life in prison and who receives the ultimate punishment. The numbers, however, tell a different story. They confirm the terrible truth that bias and discrimination warp our nation's judicial system at the very time it matters most—in matters of life and death. The factors that determine who will live and who will die—race, sex, and geography—are the very same ones that blind justice was meant to ignore. This prejudicial distribution should be a moral outrage to every American.

THE WHERE AND HOW OF EXECUTIONS

On September 1, 1995, legislation reinstituting the death penalty went into effect in New York, bringing the total number of states with the death penalty to 38. Sadly, the list of states that do not employ capital punishment seems woefully short: Alaska, Hawaii, Iowa, Maine, Massachusetts, Michigan, Minnesota, North Dakota, Rhode Island, Vermont, West Virginia, Wisconsin, and the District of Columbia remain the only jurisdictions that have not adopted legal murder.

Between 1976, when the Supreme Court reinstated the use of capital punishment, and June 1996, 330 death row inmates have been executed. Over that period, the number of executions per year has generally risen. After a slow start—there were no executions in 1976 and only one in 1977—the rate started rising rapidly. Every year since 1984, the number of condemned prisoners executed has been in the double digits, with a high of 56 in 1995. With concerted efforts in the states and in Congress to cut off death row appeals, it appears that each new year will see a new record for executions.

The methods used and frequency of executions vary widely from state to state. Far and away the most popular methods are lethal injection, authorized by 32 states and used in 193 executions; and electrocution, legal in 11 states and used in 123 executions. A distant third is the gas chamber, an option in seven states and used in nine executions. Although we deceive ourselves if we believe there are humane ways to take life, it seems particularly barbaric that four states authorize hanging and have carried out three executions in this manner; and that two states, Idaho and Utah, sanction execution by firing squad, with two executions having been performed this way.

GEOGRAPHY AND THE DEATH PENALTY

Murders committed in certain regions of our country are much more likely to result in the death penalty than are murders in other regions. The southern states (Alabama, Arkansas, Florida, Georgia, Louisiana, Mississippi, North Carolina, Oklahoma, South Carolina, Texas, Virginia) are host to a disproportionate percentage of executions. Home to roughly 26 percent of our nation's population, these states have carried out 83 percent of our nation's executions since 1976. If you commit murder in a southern state, you are roughly three times more likely to be executed for the crime there as elsewhere. In contrast, the northeastern states have a much larger population, generally lower murder rates, and accounted for only two executions (both in Pennsylvania), or less than 1 percent of the executions since 1976.

Texas—which accounts for little more than 6 percent of the nation's population—has executed 106 death row inmates, or a staggering 32 percent of the national total. Despite this liberal use of the death penalty, the state's murder rate is 25 percent higher than the national average—in 1992, 12.7 per 100,000 compared to 9.3 per 100,000 nationwide.

Thus, after 20 years of the highest rate of execution in the country, Texas continues to outpace the rest of the country in its rate of murder. This explodes the myth of capital punishment being an effective deterrent. It also gives us a glimpse of how unevenly and in many cases prejudicially capital punishment is applied.

RACE AND THE DEATH PENALTY

The relationship between race and capital punishment is much more complex than most people suppose. One surprise for many people is that more white defendants than black defendants have been executed. Since 1976, according to the Death Penalty Information Center, 56 percent of the condemned prisoners executed have been white, 38 percent have been black, and 6 percent have been Hispanic, Native American, or Asian. And death row population statistics reflect similar percentages. As of January 1996, 48 percent of the inmates on death row were white, 41 percent were black, 7.5 percent were Hispanic, and 3.5 percent were listed as "other." (See *Death Row, U.S.A.*, NAACP Legal Defense Fund.)

These statistics are simply the beginning of a chain that is not generally reported by the media, and so is not known by the public. Numerous researchers have shown conclusively that African American defendants are far more likely to receive the death penalty than are white defendants charged with the same crime. For instance, African Americans make up 25 percent of Alabama's population, yet of Alabama's 117 death row inmates, 43 percent are black. Indeed, 71 percent of the people executed there since the resumption of capital punishment have been black.

The population of Georgia's Middle Judicial Circuit is 40 percent black, but 77 percent of the circuit's capital decisions have been found against black defendants. The Ocmulgee Judicial Circuit posts remarkably similar numbers. In 79 percent of the cases in which the district attorney sought the death penalty, the defendant was black, despite the fact that only 44 percent of the circuit's population is black. More ominously, in the cases where black defendants faced capital prosecution, 90 percent of the district attorney's peremptory strikes were used to keep African Americans off the juries.

And this disproportion in capital sentencing is not just a Southern problem, for the results of the 1988 federal law providing for a death penalty for drug kingpins are telling. In 1993, all nine defendants approved for capital prosecution were African Americans. Of the first 36 cases in which prosecutors sought the death penalty under this new legislation, four of the defendants were white, four were Hispanic, and 28 were black. (See the Racial Justice Act, Y1.1/8 103-458.)

It's Not That You Kill, It's Who You Kill

It is not just the race of the defendant that affects the state's decision of whether to seek the death penalty and whether it is meted out. The race of the victim—more specifically, whether or not the victim was white—can have an even stronger influence.

Dr. David Baldus of the University of Iowa has studied over 2,500 Georgia murder cases. Controlling for 230 nonracial factors in the cases, he found that defendants accused of murdering a white victim are 4.3 times more likely to receive the death penalty than defendants accused of killing blacks. Baldus determined that the race of the murderer was less important than the race of the victim. Fewer than 40 percent of the homicide victims in Georgia are white, yet fully 87 percent of the cases resulting in the death penalty involved white victims.

Baldus cited one judicial circuit in Georgia where, despite the fact that 65 percent of the homicide cases involved African American victims, 85 percent of the cases in which the district attorney sought the death penalty were against murderers of whites. Overall, this particular district attorney sought the death penalty in 34 percent of the cases involving white victims but a mere 5.8 percent of the cases in which the victim was black. (See the Racial Justice Act, Y1.1/8 103-458.)

Georgia is not the only state where the color of the victim's skin can mean the difference between life and death. Nationwide, even though 50 percent of murder victims are African American, says the Death Penalty Information Center, almost 85 percent of the victims in death penalty cases are white. And in their 1989 book *Death and Discrimination: Racial Disparities in Capital Sentencing,* Samuel Gross and Robert Mauro analyzed sentencing in capital cases in Arkansas, Florida, Georgia, Illinois, Mississippi, North Carolina, Oklahoma, and Virginia during a period when these states accounted for 379 of the 1,011 death penalties nationwide. They found widespread discrepancies in sentencing based on the *victim's* race in all eight states.

Defendants in Florida, for example, who killed whites

received the death penalty eight times more often than those defendants convicted of killing African Americans. In Bay County, blacks are the victims of 40 percent of the murders, yet in all 17 cases between 1975 and 1987 in which a death sentence was handed down, the victims were white.

As one study after another confirmed the correlation between the race of the homicide victim and whether the defendant would receive a capital sentence, the evidence became so overwhelming that Congress's General Accounting Office decided to take up the question itself. In its February 1990 report *Death Penalty Sentencing*, the GAO reviewed 28 studies based on 23 sets of data and concluded, "In eighty-two percent of the studies, race of the victim was found to influence the likelihood of being charged with capital murder or receiving the death penalty, i.e., those who murdered whites were found more likely to be sentenced to death than those who murdered blacks."

And when a case involves interracial murder, the bias against black homicide defendants multiplies the effects of the bias against the murderers of white victims. Since 1976, only four white defendants have been executed for killing a black person, yet 75 black defendants have been executed for murdering a white person. Astoundingly, African Americans who murder whites are *19 times as likely to be executed* as whites who kill blacks.

* * *

103

In 1987, Warren McClesky, a black man armed with formidable evidence linking the victim's race with the distribution of the death penalty, appealed to the Supreme Court to overturn his death sentence. He argued that the fact his victim was white played an important role in his sentencing. Although the Court acknowledged that the correlation of the victim's race and the imposition of the death penalty was "statistically significant in the system as a whole" (*McClesky v. Kemp*, 481 U.S. 279), it denied McClesky's petition saying that the burden is on the defendant to prove his individual sentence was based on his victim's race. (See Smolowe, "Race and the Death Penalty," *Time*, April 29, 1991.) McClesky was executed on September 25, 1991.

In response to the *McClesky* decision, the Racial Justice Act was introduced in Congress in 1994. The purpose of the act was to allow condemned prisoners to appeal their death sentences using evidence of past discriminatory sentencing—the kind of evidence that failed to save McClesky. After passing in the House 217-212, the bill failed in the Senate. To date, there has been no precedent set for citing biased sentencing patterns to successfully appeal a death sentence.

With black men nearly eight times more likely to be victims of homicide than white men, could there be a more blatant message from the criminal justice system that it values some lives more highly than others? Not in a loud voice that would attract undue attention, but quietly and methodically, one prosecution at a time, our judicial system is telling us that African American life is less important than white life, and its annihilation less tragic. Our judicial system is demonstrably, institutionally racist in the end result, and the end result—killing a disproportionate number of black males—matters.

GENDER AND THE DEATH PENALTY

North Carolina prison officials described Velma Barfield as a model prisoner. She read the Bible daily and offered support and counsel to younger inmates. Properly diagnosed and treated, the bipolar behavior that had plagued Barfield was under control, and she was making a life for herself in prison.

But Velma Barfield was a condemned woman. In 1978, she was convicted of murdering her fiancé, Stuart Taylor, and confessed to the arsenic poisonings of three others, including her mother. She received the death penalty for her crime. Six years later, on November 2, 1984, after numerous appeals to delay her execution failed, her time had come.

In her final words, she expressed her remorse. "I want to say that I am sorry for all the hurt that I have caused. I know that everybody has gone through a lot of pain, all the families connected, and I am sorry, and I want to thank everybody who has supported me all these six years." After a last meal of cola and cheese puffs, Barfield was dressed in a pair of pink pajamas and was strapped onto a gurney and given a sleep-inducing drug. Fifteen minutes after North Carolina prison officials administered a lethal dose of procuronium bromide, this 52-year-old grandmother became the first woman executed since the Supreme Court reinstated the death penalty in 1976. (See Schmidt, "Woman Executed in North Carolina," *New York Times*, November 2, 1984.) To this date, she is also the last woman executed.

That only one woman has been executed in the last 20 years has prompted more than one legal scholar to suggest that female homicide defendants benefit from preferential discrimination. The most notable critic has been the late Justice Marshall who, in his concurring opinion in *Furman v. Georgia*, rhetorically asked what other explanation could be given for the discrepancy between the number of women who commit murder and the much smaller number who receive the death penalty.

Data in the FBI's Supplementary Homicide Reports state that about 14 percent of all known murder and non-negligent manslaughter suspects are women. However, as of January 1996, only 1.6 percent of the inmates on death row are women, according to *Death Row, U.S.A.*

Elizabeth Rapaport is one of the few researchers studying gender and the death penalty. She cites two legitimate factors that influence women's lower rate of capital punishment: prior criminal record and seriousness of the offense (the violence and brutality with which the murder was committed). Prior conviction for a violent felony is one factor that may lead a prosecutor to seek a capital trial. Twenty percent of male defendants have a

106

history of violent felony convictions, whereas only 4 percent of female defendants have such a history. Women are also substantially less likely to commit murders with excessive force and brutality or with multiple victims.

Rapaport estimates that if men and women were judged equally—i.e., if only the circumstances that should legitimately influence the prosecution and sentencing in a case, such as prior record and excessive cruelty, were considered—we should expect about 4 percent of death row inmates to be women. The difference between that figure and the current percentage of women on death row suggests that women accused of murder may be as much as two-and-a-half times less likely to face capital punishment because of their gender.

Other evidence points to another twist in the tale of capital punishment. It appears that a woman's relationship to her victim may influence the punishment she receives, just as the race of the victim does.

Overall, homicide defendants are much more likely to receive the death penalty for the murder of strangers for economic gain than they are for the murder of intimate family members—including children—in anger. Once again, the gravity of the crime seems to depend upon the identity of its victim. (Eighty percent of the victims of predatory murder are men, while women are six times more likely than men to be murdered by an intimate.)

However, the statistical tables are turned concerning women who take the life of a spouse or a close family member. Women who kill those who are close to them

107

are more likely to receive the ultimate penalty than men who kill those close to them. In North Carolina, for example, a man who kills a stranger is twice as likely to receive the death penalty as a man who kills an intimate or a family member. But the percentage of women on death row who have killed intimates much more closely resembles the rate at which women kill those close to them: 65 percent of the murders women commit are against intimates, and 49 percent of the women on death row killed spouses or family members. (See Rapaport, "The Death Penalty and Gender Discrimination," *Law and Society Review* 25, 1991.) Surely, it seems that our society's continued assignment to women of the roles of nurturers and keepers of the family that influences our judicial system to deem women's murdering of family members as somehow more reprehensible—or more dangerous—than the same offenses committed by men.

My goal is not to question whether killing a loved one or a stranger is the more heinous crime. Taking any life is a terrible matter. Nor do I wish to suggest that more women should be executed for the murders they commit. Rather, my purpose is to point out that women who kill are held to different standards than are men who kill. Whether these standards are prejudicial for them or against them, the point is that they *are* different. Gender joins race and geography as another factor by which the death penalty is inflicted differentially and prejudicially.

* * *

We are confronted with the undeniable evidence that the death penalty is handed down unjustly. The reaction of most state governments to this evidence has been to assert that the death penalty is still necessary, and that what is needed is a way of ensuring that it is distributed fairly and handed down for the right reasons. At this time, the Supreme Court agrees with the majority of the states. The goal of implementing a fair system for imposing the death penalty, however, has proved very elusive. And the statistics that are proving the failure of this policy have been produced under the supposedly stricter post-*Furman* laws.

Thirty-five years in the civil rights struggle has taught me that you can't legislate acceptance, objectivity, or morality. How then, at the moment between life and death, is society to erase a lifetime of social conditioning, assumptions, and attitudes the judges and jurors may not even realize they hold? There is no way the states, the federal government, or the judicial system can ensure that every prosecuting attorney, every jury member, and every judge involved in every homicide case is impartial and unbiased. And in the case of the death penalty, the stakes are just too high for even one life to be lost to prejudice and hatred.

6

DETERRENCE, BRUTALIZATION, AND SNOWSTORMS

I n broad daylight on January 17, 1977, a man was standing by a wall when six men raised their guns and shot at him. Five bullets tore through the man's chest, penetrating his heart and killing him instantly. The men who shot him, their job done, left the scene as quickly as they could.

This was no drive-by shooting—it was the execution of convicted murderer Gary Gilmore, authorized by the state of Utah and implemented by a six-man firing squad. Each sharpshooter on the squad was issued one round for his rifle, and one of those cartridges was a blank so that no one would know who was actually the executioner.

Gilmore's was the first execution to take place after the Supreme Court's reinstitution of the death penalty in 1976, the first execution in the United States in nearly a decade. Thus, it was the focus of an unprecedented amount of media attention. In the months leading up to the execution, the national media debated his case on television news programs, in *Time* and *Newsweek*, and in newspapers across America. On the fateful day, Gilmore's story led off each of the major networks' evening broadcasts.

The executions following Gilmore's did not attract the same attention. Even though the implementation of the death penalty is anything but commonplace, each subsequent execution seemed to be of less and less interest.

Psychology professor Sam McFarland saw these first executions as his opportunity to test the claim of death penalty supporters that the fear of receiving the ultimate sanction deterred would-be criminals from committing murder. The first four executions after reinstitution occurred between 1977 and 1981. McFarland analyzed the weekly homicide rates in the months following these executions and found that in the two weeks following Gilmore's execution, national homicide rates were significantly below average. However, the next three executions had no perceptible effect on the murder rate.

A less-thorough researcher might have concluded that the results confirmed a deterrent factor that was dependent on public awareness, but McFarland searched for other factors. He determined that Gilmore's execution coincided with some of the worst winter weather to hit the eastern half of the country in years. Blizzards blanketed the East Coast as far south as Georgia and Alabama, and the mercury plunged far below normal in the January weeks immediately after Gilmore's execution.

When he examined his data regionally, McFarland found a sharp drop in homicides in the Northeast and the South during the exceptionally inclement period, but in western states experiencing normal weather patterns, homicide rates were at their usual levels. Gilmore's execution didn't deter potential killers, several feet of snow and bitter wind chills did. McFarland published his findings in an article entitled "Is Capital Punishment a Short-Term Deterrent to Homicide?" in the *Journal of Criminal Law and Criminology* in 1983.

Dr. McFarland's snowstorm acts as a parable illuminating the question of deterrence and the death penalty. Human behavior—especially the unspeakable act of taking another life—is far too complex to be linked to any one variable. It's too simplistic to say that the death penalty discourages people from committing murder or that eliminating the death penalty would drive the homicide rate up. Murder is a profoundly emotional crime. It can result from intense and fiery rage, the all-encompassing despair of poverty and debilitating hopelessness, mental imbalance, or simple depravity. Seldom is murder a calm and rational decision.

DETERRENCE THEORY

In the modern debate, deterrence has emerged as the only morally palatable argument for the death penalty. Seeking vengeance for its own sake against cold-blooded killers or saving precious tax dollars is difficult to argue directly, but the basic logic of deterrence—sacrificing the lives of a few cruel and dangerous murderers in order to save innocent lives—resonates powerfully with the American people.

Deterrence theory is predicated on the seemingly common-sense notion that the possibility of receiving the death penalty will deter would-be killers, whereas the possibility of receiving a sentence of life in prison without possibility of parole will not. If murderers were rational people educated in the laws of the states in which they live, the theory might have some weight. For criminals to be deterred by the penalty, they both must know the possible penalties in the state in which they commit their crimes and must rationally weigh the risks and benefits of their actions.

Most homicides, however, are unplanned, impulsive acts by one person against another person. The emotionally charged environment in which these crimes take place do not suggest a coolly calculating murderer weighing his options.

If a murderer were to sit down to calculate the odds of being punished for a premeditated act of violence, this is what he would have to consider. In the United States, the death penalty is handed down for only about 1 out of every 100 homicides. In capital cases, the rate is higher, but it is still only 6-15 per 100 offenses (depending on the state), and of those sentenced, only 6 per 100 are executed. With these odds, the threat of being killed by the planned victim or in a confrontation with police is a much more realistic threat than the distant and abstract possibility of execution—but those more immediate threats have yet to eliminate the violent crime in our streets. (See Roger Hood, *The Death Penalty: A World-Wide Perspective*, 1990.) In fact, a 1980 study by William Bowers and Glenn Pierce titled "Deterrence or Brutalization: What Is the Effect of Executions?" and published in the journal *Crime and Delinquency*, showed that the primary distinguishing characteristic between those imprisoned for homicide and those imprisoned for the lesser charge of aggravated assault was that the victims of the former were unarmed or intoxicated. Neither the killers' intent nor any deterrence by laws played a major part.

Many proponents of the deterrence principle truly want to believe that greater and swifter use of the death penalty will save innocent lives. In the frightening world of senseless and seemingly uncontrollable crime in which we live, their wishful thinking is understandable. But, it is just wishful thinking. Many years of research by sociologists, criminologists, psychologists, and others, have been invested on this topic, but no one has been able to prove that the death penalty deters would-be killers.

EARLY RESEARCH

Early in the twentieth century, American social scientists

began to investigate the possibility that the death penalty had a deterrent effect. They compared homicide rates in states that had abolished the death penalty to rates in neighboring states that continued to use capital punishment. Five decades of research across the country failed to show a higher murder rate in states that had abolished the death penalty.

A number of researchers also took a look at states that had either abolished the death penalty or had reinstated its use after a period of abolition. In startling contradiction to what deterrence theory predicts, these studies found that murder rates were stable—they did not rise after a state stopped using capital punishment, nor did they decline when a state reintroduced capital punishment.

Among the most careful and technically sophisticated of this early work was Thorsten Sellin's research in New England and the Midwest. Sellin studied five groups of contiguous states chosen for their similarities in social organization, composition of population, economic and social conditions, and other factors. In each group, the major difference amongst the states was that at least one of the states used the death penalty and the others did not. Looking at the years 1940-1955, Dr. Sellin found that the average homicide rate in these states was in no way related to whether or not the state sanctioned execution as a punishment. (See Hood, *The Death Penalty: A World-Wide Perspective*.)

EHRLICH'S BOMBSHELL

It is against this backdrop that Isaac Ehrlich's 1975 study "The Deterrent Effect of Capital Punishment: A Question of Life and Death" caused so much controversy. In his study he analyzed annual national homicide and execution rates from 1933 until 1970. Using a sophisticated new statistical method developed for use with computers and controlling for a number of other factors that contribute to the homicide rate—such as unemployment, age distribution, and per capita income—Ehrlich found a deterrent factor. Based on his numbers, Ehrlich boldly estimated that each execution deterred between seven and eight homicides. (See Archer, Gartner, and Beittel, "Homicide and the Death Penalty: A Cross-National Test of a Deterrence Hypothesis," *Journal of Criminal Law and Criminology*, 1983.)

Ehrlich's results triggered controversy and spurred additional research. Another researcher, Dr. Yunker, quickly weighed in on Ehrlich's side, exclaiming wildly that it was really 156 innocent lives saved per execution rather than Ehrlich's much more conservative estimate. (As cited in McFarland, "Is Capital Punishment a Short-Term Deterrent to Homicide?")

In the years that followed, scientists have reanalyzed Ehrlich's data but have failed to replicate his results. This has led a number of them to criticize his methods. For example, researchers using an econometric model, a newer and more powerful statistical procedure, concluded that Ehrlich's data did not support his results. Another researcher, Dr. Layson, refined Ehrlich's social and economic controls on poverty, educational levels, and family structures. These refinements appeared to account for the "deterrent factor" that Ehrlich had supposedly found. (Archer, Gartner, and Beittel, "Homicide and the Death Penalty: A Cross-National Test of a Deterrence Hypothesis.")

One of the most damaging charges against Ehrlich's methodology was that by lumping together statistics from all of the states, he masked significant differences in rates between states, specifically between states maintaining the death penalty and those that had abolished the death penalty.

Other researchers designed new studies. Using a research design similar to Sellin's and taking advantage of modern statistical models, William Bailey compared the homicide rates in states with the death penalty with the rates in states that did not have the death penalty. Controlling for socioeconomic and demographic variables, as well as for levels of aggravated assault, Bailey found that states continuing to use the death penalty had higher murder rates than states that had abolished it— except in the state of Utah. (Archer, Gartner, and Beittel, "Homicide and the Death Penalty: A Cross-National Test of a Deterrence Hypothesis.") Bailey found that in Utah, "a one percent increase in the certainty of the death penalty is associated with an approximate reduction in homicides of only eight-hundredths of a person per 100,000 population." That means that if Utah doubled its rate of execution, it might save eight-tenths of a person. (Hood, *The Death Penalty: A World-Wide Perspective*.) Not exactly strong support for Ehrlich's findings.

SHORT-TERM DETERRENCE

Rather than study the possibility that the death penalty deterred homicide over the long term, researcher David Phillips hypothesized that perhaps executions produced a short-term deterrence measurable in days or weeks rather than years. After studying the weekly homicide statistics before and after 22 highly publicized executions in England that took place in the years just before that country's abolition of the death penalty, Phillips found that in the two weeks following each execution, homicide rates fell to nearly 35 percent below average. In the third to fifth weeks after the execution, however, homicides rebounded to above-normal levels, erasing the deterrent effect of the first two weeks. (McFarland, "Is Capital Punishment a Short-Term Deterrent to Homicide?")

In his next study, Phillips turned his attention to the United States. He and John Hensley studied murder rates following highly publicized death penalties handed down in white-victim murder cases. Their results were mixed. They did isolate a four-day period of lower murder rates against white victims after the sentencings, but were unable to determine if the deterrent factor of a death penalty sentencing was greater than an equally well-publicized sentence of life in prison. (Hood, *The Death Penalty: A World-Wide Perspective.*)

MURDER AND EXECUTION IN CHICAGO

As the sallies between Ehrlich and his supporters and their critics subsided into an uneasy stalemate, William Bailey came back on the scene. He concluded that one of the major problems with Ehrlich's work resulted from the data he had to use. Ehrlich, and nearly all the researchers before him, had studied the effect of executions on homicide rates. The only homicides, however, that are prosecuted as capital cases are first-degree, or premeditated, murders. Following the deterrence model—in which the potential murderer knows that he might get the death penalty—any real deterrent effect should be recognizable in first-degree murders. But no previous researcher studied the relationship between premeditated murder and the death penalty because no government or private organization collects nationwide data on first-degree murders. Researchers had to rely on either general homicide records from the U.S. Public Health Service or murder and non-negligent manslaughter numbers from the FBI.

Bailey also faulted Ehrlich on using national homicide rates, which did not distinguish between significantly higher rates in some states than in others. Bailey doubted that even the state would be the ideal geographic unit to use: within each state, different jurisdictions have wildly

119

varying homicide rates and socioeconomic conditions.

In what at first seems like an unlikely choice of data, Bailey attempted to rectify these problems by studying first-degree murder rates and executions in Chicago between 1915 and 1921. It seems unorthodox that he would turn to 60-year-old statistics, but the Chicago data provided an excellent resolution to the problems of Ehrlich's data. Accurate first-degree murder records were available for the period in question. Examining the rates for Chicago alone prevented the cloaking effect state or national figures introduced and allowed Bailey to more accurately control for socioeconomic factors that affect murder rates. To isolate the effect of executions, Bailey controlled for the city's population density, level of spending for social services, seasonal fluctuations in the murder rate, and the certainty of arrest and imprisonment.

In addition, all executions in this period took place right in Chicago, at the Cook County Prison. Most jurisdictions execute condemned prisoners at facilities far away from the communities in which they committed their crimes. Chicago residents, living in the shadow of the executions, would be uniquely aware of the consequences of murder and particularly open to a deterrent effect. In all these respects, Chicago was an ideal setting to test the theory of deterrence.

Bailey found no evidence to support the claim that executions lowered the murder rate. More often than not, he found that executions were linked to a higher murder rate. Bailey also studied the effect of the executions on

120

the general homicide rate, as the earlier research had done, and found similar results. (Bailey, "Disaggregation in Deterrence and Death Penalty Research: The Case of Murder in Chicago," *Journal of Criminal Law and Criminology* 74, 1983.)

POLICE KILLINGS

In a separate study, Bailey set about testing another tenet of the deterrence theory—that the death penalty provides additional protection for law enforcement officers. Proponents of capital punishment have long argued that only the threat of the death penalty can protect police officers by deterring criminals from using deadly weapons to commit crimes or to resist arrest. They contend that without the death penalty a criminal who has already committed a crime punishable by life imprisonment has nothing to lose by killing an officer attempting to make the arrest. Again, it seems highly unlikely that in the heat of confrontation, criminals will be thinking about anything but getting away, but protecting law enforcement officers remains a popular reason cited in support of the death penalty.

In Bailey's first look at the possible deterrent effect executions might have on police killings, he examined data from 1961 through 1971. He did not find any evidence to support the contention that executions lowered the number of police officers killed or afforded them any additional protection. He did note that an

121

important factor in the study which he could not control for was public opinion. During the 1960s, the death penalty was under intense attack for moral reasons and by critics who were deeply skeptical of its effectiveness. As a result, judges and juries were handing down such penalties with less and less frequency. Bailey feared that his study may have measured public opinion and cultural messages about the death penalty rather than its ability—or inability—to protect law enforcement officers.

To check this theory, Bailey studied the same relationship during a different period. The second era he studied, 1973 through 1984, saw a marked shift in the social and political discussion about the death penalty. Public support for the death penalty was increasing dramatically, and the 1976 Supreme Court case *Gregg v. Georgia* reinstated capital punishment.

At first, Bailey seemed to find some effect in this period. The rate of police killings were highest during the three years prior to the court's reinstitution of the death penalty and declined steadily after *Gregg*. The only exception to this pattern was an increase in 1979, followed by a sharp decline in 1980.

Statistics, however—especially national figures—sometimes lie. After controlling for the usual sociodemographics, Bailey found that police officers were no safer in death-penalty states than in death penalty-free states. He also found that the states with the highest levels of capital punishment did not in fact have lower rates of police killings, also contradicting the predictions of deterrence proponents. (Bailey and Peterson, "Police Killings and Capital Punishment: The Post-*Furman* Period," *Criminology* 25, 1987.)

BRUTALIZATION THEORY

Approximately 150 years ago, the first American to systematically study whether capital punishment deterred others from committing murder came to the conclusion that it did not. Robert Rantoul, working in the 1840s, believed that by devaluing human life and sanctioning an official policy of vengeance, the death penalty actually increased the violence in society and, hence, the murder rate.

A Massachusetts state representative, Rantoul addressed his colleagues in the state legislature in the 1846 debate on public executions. Answering his opponents, Rantoul presented his evidence that disputed their claims of deterrence. He explained that in nations such as England and France where the proportion of executions to convictions was much smaller than in Massachusetts—and also much smaller than the rate in those countries 50 years before—the murder rate was actually decreasing. He had also studied the murder and execution rates in Belgium and noted that the three years in which there were more than 50 executions a year were followed by the three most murderous years in Belgium's history. (Bowers and Pierce, "Deterrence or Brutalization: What Is the Effect of Executions?")

123

More than 100 years later, with a modern array of research tools at their disposal, Bowers and Pierce came to the same conclusion as Rantoul. The two men analyzed New York State's homicide records between 1907 and 1963, and found an average increase of two to three homicides in the months following executions.

Bowers and Pierce—considering their results as well as the conflicting results of researchers attempting to prove the deterrence theory—formulated a theory of their own: the brutalization theory. The violence of officially sponsored state executions brutalizes the sensibilities of society and actually increases the murder rate by loosening the inhibitions of potential murderers and offering the example of sanctioned vengeance.

Deterrence depends on would-be murderers identifying with the executed killer. The problem with that logic is that countless psychological studies show that we identify with those whom we admire or envy. Condemned prisoners who arrive at the electric chair are a wretched lot. Since they are generally loners and social outcasts who are uneducated and have committed brutal and cowardly crimes, it is highly unlikely that calculating killers would identify with them. The contrast they see between themselves and the condemned may actually lead prospective killers to determine that the death penalty is reserved only for people unlike themselves.

The associations that do take place are a sort of "villain identification." The would-be murderer identifies the executed killer with someone who has gravely offended or threatened him, and thus sees himself in his crime as an executioner administering justice. The lesson the murderer takes from the execution is that killing someone whose actions you despise and abhor is not only acceptable but officially sanctioned.

As historical evidence, Bowers and Pierce recalled a horrifying and shameful era in our nation's past—the lynching of black men by white mobs. Since 1890, nearly 3,500 lynchings have been documented, even though lynching a person was a capital crime in many of the states in which they occurred. (So much for deterrence.) The chillingly execution-like scene of an angry white mob leading a shackled "prisoner" to the noose certainly tells me that it wasn't the condemned prisoners the vicious mobs were identifying with during these "official" executions.

Although I do not pretend to be a social scientist, the brutalization theory speaks to me and to the violence in our society in a way the deterrence theory does not. It begins to explain the unexplainable: the horrible deaths of thousands of people at the hands of wrathful mobs for imagined wrongs and misdeeds. Today I think about the articles recounting far too many urban shootings. How many times are the senseless slayings described as "execution-style"? Have our young people fallen prey to the same degraded mentality as the ugly lynch mobs of our not-so-distant past?

As I step back and consider the common-sense appeal the brutalization theory holds for me, I remember Dr.

125

McFarland's snowstorm. Just as it is too easy to say that the death penalty will keep people from killing one another, it is probably too easy to say that it makes them kill one another. Eliminating the death penalty will not check the flow of handguns or illegal drugs into our communities. Nor will it create new jobs or offer a glimmer of hope to the desperate and dispossessed. No one solution will reduce the terrifying rate of violent crime in urban centers across the country.

Scientific investigation will probably never be able to tell us conclusively if the violence of the death penalty contributes to the violence of our society. The difference between accepting the deterrence principle and accepting the brutalization principle, however, is the burden of proof each requires society to bear. If we as a society continue to impose the ultimate sanction on those who take the lives of others based on the belief that this will save lives, we need to have absolute, undeniable, incontrovertible proof that deterrence really works. The moral responsibility in deciding the fate of another human being is simply too great for anything less. My investigation into decades of deterrence research reveals that there is no such evidence. Not even close.

7

POOR MAN'S PENALTY
LACK OF REPRESENTATION

Them's that got the capital don't get the punishment.
—Mumia Abu-Jamal,
Pennsylvania death row inmate

I n 1932, in Scottsboro, Alabama, seven young black men were sentenced to death under questionable circumstances. After reviewing the abysmal legal work of the two lawyers who represented these men and the hostility in the community surrounding this case, the Supreme Court ruled that the defendents "did not have the aid of counsel in any real sense." In *Powell v. Alabama*, the Court established the precedent that any person facing capital punishment who is too poor to afford an attorney has the right to have an attorney assigned to him.

127

It was not until 30 years later, during the Kennedy administration, that all the people of the United States received the right to appointed counsel in any felony case if they could not afford one. And the Supreme Court would not have made this ruling if it hadn't decided to accept a handwritten petition from Clarence Earl Gideon, a prisoner in Florida. Although Gideon was poor, he understood the Sixth Amendment—"In all criminal prosecutions, the accused shall . . . have the assistance of counsel for his defense." It took this nation 187 years to make that promise in the Constitution available to all citizens, even indigent criminal defendants.

In the three decades that we have had court-appointed counsel, the standards for representation have varied drastically. In many states, overworked and under-paid public defenders have no choice but to represent defendants in a hurried fashion. Often the defendant's counsel will meet the defendant for the first time at the arraignment, at which the all-important decision to plead guilty or not guilty is made, and at which the state will ask for bail or that bail be denied.

As capital prosecutions reach record numbers, the system of representation for those facing the death penalty is in a state of crisis. Despite the image of slick defense lawyers that the O.J. Simpson trial, *L.A. Law*, and other televised programs project, many capital defendants are given attorneys who fail to investigate, who fall asleep during trial or come into court drunk, who are barely out of law school, or who say nothing when their client's life is on the line. Too many states encourage this malpractice by offering inadequate pay and resources for death penalty defense. Most states allow elected judges to pick attorneys. Very often, these attorneys are picked not on the basis of experience or merit, but because they will cause the least resistance at trial.

Former death row inmates, including Andrew Golden, Federico Macias, and Gary Nelson, received poor representation at trial and could have been executed despite their innocence. In their cases, competent counsel later stepped in and reversed death sentences. Others with inadequate counsel have already been executed or remain on death row. Far too often, people, mostly poor and black, are given the death penalty not because they committed the worst crimes, but because they had the worst lawyers.

The injustice of inadequate representation in death penalty cases is an affront to the nation's commitment to equal justice under law. However, this deadly problem has been ignored for years because politicians use the death penalty as a ploy for electoral success. Red flags concerning the woeful lack of representation accorded capital criminals have been raised by a number of Supreme Court justices, including Marshall, Brennan, and Blackmun. Even Justice Sandra Day O'Connor has said, "There's probably never been a wider gulf between the need for legal services and the provision of those services. There is a great deal to be concerned about, or even ashamed of."

A GOOD CITIZEN'S NIGHTMARE

Andrew Golden is a former teacher who had never received even a traffic ticket. He had been married to his wife, Ardelle, for 24 years, sharing a close relationship. He adored his two sons, Chip and Darin. That is why life on death row was so difficult for Golden, almost driving him to suicide. He kept his sanity by making things for his sons and helping them with their college applications— and by fighting to prove his innocence.

Golden was sent to death row in 1991 for allegedly drowning his wife. The case against him was absurdly weak: His wife and the family car were found in a lake at the end of a boat ramp in Winter Haven, Florida. Even the police and the medical examiner felt the evidence did not suggest foul play.

However, Golden's attorney did almost nothing to prepare for trial, assuming that the case would be thrown out beforehand. When the case was announced for trial it was too late for him to prepare—there was not enough time for an accident reconstruction. The attorney put on no defense. He failed to present the jury with a reasonable explanation for Ardelle Golden's suicide, even though she was severely depressed over her father's recent death and had four of his death notices with her in the car. The prosecutor's theory was that Golden pushed his wife off the dock to collect insurance money. The defense never mentioned to the jury that the water by the dock was not even over Ardelle's head.

With no reasonable evidence of doubt presented, the jury accepted the prosecutor's presentation of the facts and convicted Golden of first-degree murder.

Golden hired a new lawyer and had his conviction overturned by a unanimous Florida Supreme Court. Golden's trial lawyer was publicly reprimanded by the Florida bar, and Golden is suing him for malpractice. Golden was saved because he had the resources to hire his own lawyer and undo the malpractice of the trial attorney. But what about the 90 percent of defendants who are unable to afford their own counsel?

POOR SCHLUP

Lloyd Schlup may not have been quite as sympathetic a character as Andrew Golden, but he was no less innocent. Schlup was accused of a murder that took place while he was incarcerated. Despite an enormous amount of evidence of innocence, including a videotape and eyewitnesses proving that he was nowhere near the scene of the crime, Schlup came within an hour of his execution. Unlike the daily visits by Robert Shapiro to O.J. Simpson, Schlup's trial attorney visited him twice for a total of 75 minutes before trial. They never talked on the phone. Despite his failure to interview any of the 20 witnesses who saw the murder, the attorney was paid $2,000 for representation. The 1985 murder trial took two days, and Schlup was convicted.

After he was sent back to jail for this crime, new

counsel came in to represent Schlup and presented 20 affidavits from eyewitnesses testifying to Schlup's innocence. The governor of Missouri stopped Schlup's execution to allow time to review the case for possible clemency. The Missouri Resource Center also came to Schlup's aid and helped to halt the impending execution.

THE PHILADELPHIA STORY

Poor people facing society's ultimate penalty have to rely on public funds for representation. Yet, in more and more jurisdictions, public services of all kinds are being slashed for lack of funds. Lloyd Schlup would probably be dead now if the Missouri Resource Center had not been available to help him get his day in court. Now the Missouri Center, as well as agencies in other states set up to help the indigent in legal matters, are threatened because there is a growing movement in Congress to cut their funding. Equal justice under law is but an empty slogan when the resources so fundamental to its attainment are unavailable.

A dramatic and graphic example of this nationwide problem is occurring in Philadelphia, Pennsylvania. In the birthplace of American liberty, justice is becoming ever more just another commodity available only to the few who can afford it. This is strikingly evident in the disparity between what is provided versus what is needed to represent adequately those facing the death penalty. A brief look at what is happening there reveals that, when resources are scarce, the constitutional protections that distinguish our system of government are the first to be jettisoned.

According to a 1991 survey by the National Association of Counties, fully 40 percent of counties in the country with populations exceeding 100,000 face major budgetary shortfalls. All of them have been forced to trim away resources required for equal justice to prevail. At the top of the list of resource-strapped counties is Philadelphia.

While already inadequate funding for indigent defense programs is being slashed across the nation in the face of shrinking state revenues, Pennsylvania provides no funds at all for such defense. Philadelphia itself has no organized system to provide training or support for attorneys who defend capital cases, and the public defender system, which in 1991 was finally empowered to take on up to 20 percent of indigent capital cases, has no funding for that responsibility and has had no cases assigned to it. Philadelphia does have a capital resource center, although its funding has been cut severely as the city tries to survive. This has left ill-trained, ill-prepared, inexperienced lawyers to handle the most demanding criminal cases of all.

There are almost 200 people under sentence of death in the Commonwealth of Pennsylvania. With less than 15 percent of the state's population, Philadelphia accounts for more than half of the state's condemned prisoners. One reason for this is that the Philadelphia district attorney's office seeks the death penalty in well over 50 percent of all homicides, or about 300 cases a year. This requires defense counsel to prepare to defend against a capital charge, even though it may be unwarranted by the facts.

But in cash-strapped Philadelphia, indigent defendants facing the death penalty are represented by neither the Philadelphia Defender Association (public defender) nor any other organized group of lawyers trained in the difficult and highly specialized area of capital defense. "As a result," says Philadelphia public defender Stuart Schuman, "representation in these life and death cases is usually undertaken by overworked, underpaid, court-appointed lawyers."

Only about 80 lawyers out of approximately 8,000 in the city both qualify and are willing to represent capitally charged defendants. Since most of the defendants are poor, to undertake such cases is to agree to work for little remuneration. Court-appointed lawyers are forced to wait up to two years between the time they are appointed and when they can collect their fees. They cannot even request payment until after the sentence has been affirmed by the court, a process which usually takes about 14 months. After filing for fees ($40 an hour for out-of-court time and $50 for in-court—a fraction of what a competent Philadelphia attorney can bill a private client), not only do they have to wait up to another year to be paid, their billable time is often cut. As one respected defense attorney describes it, "We extend credit to the city for two years, so it's no wonder that most lawyers just process cases."

When compensation is both insufficient and belated, experienced death penalty lawyers become extremely reluctant to take new capital cases. They know the amount of time necessary to prepare and present a decent defense. "A system being held together on the backs of counsel having to beg and borrow is guaranteed to provide second-rate representation," says experienced Philadelphia trial lawyer Samuel Stretton. "The best lawyers don't do them any more."

While it may be hard to summon sympathy for attorneys, the real victims of such a system are the very rights and protections we take for granted as distinguishing our form of government. Ironically, when these protections are sacrificed in the interest of cost and expediency, much larger expenditures of resources are implicated down the line.

In testimony on behalf of the American Bar Association, Columbia University law professor James S. Liebman reported to Congress on the findings of the ABA Task Force on Death Penalty Habeas Corpus:

> Poor compensation almost inevitably means that only inexperienced and ill-prepared lawyers will be available to handle capital cases, and that lawyers will not develop expertise because they will be financially unable to handle more than one capital case. Not surprisingly, therefore, the

inexperienced and inexpert counsel who handle many of the cases frequently conduct inadequate factual investigations, are unable to keep abreast of the complex and constantly changing legal doctrines that apply in capital litigation, and mistakenly fail to make timely objections to improper procedures.

Habeas corpus is the time-honored right of the imprisoned to ensure their convictions were not tainted by unconstitutional violations by the state. As Professor Liebman explained to Congress, the findings of the ABA task force show that "the high level of constitutional error implanted in capital trials and appeals by uncompensated, inexpert, and ill-prepared counsel has required the federal courts to overturn and order retrials of more than 40 percent of the post-1976 death sentences that they have reviewed. . . . Moreover, the expensive and time-consuming proceedings necessary to uncover that astonishing number of constitutional violations and to retry and review all those cases is without doubt the single largest cause of delay in capital litigation."

Few lawyers can afford to take these court-appointed cases, which, in addition to being a great financial burden, are always emotionally draining. As Judge William Manfredi, the homicide calendar judge who determines the initial allocation of resources in death penalty trials, says, "Eighty competent attorneys out of 8,000 attorneys is outrageous."

While Judge Manfredi believes the large law firms should and could significantly increase the number of qualified attorneys willing to take such cases, they are very unlikely to do so. What is more likely is that the number will continue to shrink as overburdened lawyers remove themselves from the list, choosing to make a living instead.

While the pool of qualified defense counsel grows smaller, the number of cases the district attorney prosecutes capitally grows larger, further stretching the system. Indeed, many Philadelphia lawyers identify the DA's practice of overcharging in homicide cases as among the most pernicious aspects of Philadelphia's death penalty process.

Once the DA alerts the court that it intends to seek the death penalty, the jury must be "death qualified." This means that any prospective juror opposed to the death penalty as a matter of principle is automatically barred from serving. Once these exclusions take place, the jury that is seated is characterized by criminologists as "death prone"—far more likely to convict than a jury which includes a fair cross-section of death penalty opponents. "The indiscriminate move by prosecutors to select death qualified jurors is the real cancer in the system," says veteran defense attorney Daniel Greene.

Judge David Savitt, one of 15 Common Pleas judges in Philadelphia presiding in death penalty trials, is also concerned. "The tendency has been for the DA to death qualify the jury even when they have no intention to seek the death penalty," he says, "because they know that a death-qualified jury is a guilt-prone jury."

Experts and Investigators

In death penalty trials, juries are required to make the most important decision any citizen can be called on to make about a criminal defendant: first, is the defendant guilty of the charge of murder; and second, whether the appropriate penalty is life in prison or death. To make these critical judgments, juries have a right to know not only the detailed circumstances of the crime, but as much about the defendant as possible. Is the defendant mentally competent? Was he motivated by greed or self-interest, or did he act while under the influence of drugs or alcohol or psychosis? Is he mentally retarded or dominated by another? Are the circumstances that led to the crime likely to recur? Was the defendant responding to an abusive situation, or shaped by a lifetime of abuse? Is he remorseful?

Juries are composed of ordinary citizens with no special training or expertise in making these determinations. To do so fairly, they must rely on trained investigators and qualified medical, psychiatric, and forensic experts. The U.S. Supreme Court has held that a poor defendant is entitled to all expert services reasonably necessary for an effective defense. This really means that juries have a right to all the information they need to make informed life-or-death judgments about the defendants before them.

Given Philadelphia's financial constraints, however, the Supreme Court's prescription is impossible to fill. Judge Manfredi describes the judges' job as balancing "the competing interests of quality representation with the economic situation of Philadelphia." For the families of poor, capitally charged defendants—and the death penalty seems reserved exclusively for the poor—this balancing act allows them only to watch helplessly as their loved ones face the possibility of execution without the assistance of the experts we would all demand for ourselves or our loved ones in similar circumstances.

Anthony Reid was such a defendant. Abandoned by his parents before his first birthday and raised in poverty with seven foster brothers and sisters, Reid was charged with homicide at the age of 20. He was unable to afford counsel, and so the court appointed Samuel Stretton.

At the beginning of Reid's trial, Stretton asked that his client be examined by a psychologist, who might uncover facets of Reid's life that could help the jury get a more complete picture of the young man. Presiding Judge Albert Sabo denied the motion on the grounds that it was an unwarranted expense—at least until Reid was convicted and the jury needed to determine his appropriate sentence.

On January 9, 1991, Reid was convicted. The next day, the penalty phase began, and Stretton renewed his request for a psychological evaluation and testimony. "Your client told me . . . that he has no problems at all, so what are we going to look for?" Judge Sabo asked the startled defense attorney.

Dr. Gerald Cook, an experienced forensic psychologist, was in the courtroom at Stretton's request, ready and willing to conduct the examination of Reid.

"I want the jury to understand his personality . . . his intellect. . . . I am looking for mitigating circumstances," Stretton said.

"Why don't you dig for gold while you're at it?" Sabo interrupted.

Before ruling on Stretton's request for the expert witness, Sabo turned to the prosecuting attorney and asked his opinion. Like the judge, he too relied on the "expertise" of the 22-year-old Reid himself, who swore "under oath that he has no psychological problems."

Stretton protested. "I have retained a psychologist."

"Take care of it out of your fee," the judge replied, sarcastically. "There is no basis for me to expend public funds needlessly."

"I am court-appointed," the defense attorney protested one last time. "There is a good chance we will never be paid. . . ."

"A good chance he [the psychiatrist] would never be paid, either," Judge Sabo said, dismissing the request.

Thus, in the crucial penalty phase, during which the defendant is allowed to provide any information for the jury to consider in mitigation of the sentence, the jury heard only the predictable pleas for mercy of Mr. Reid's foster sisters, begging for his life.

"I am just asking for his life, just don't take his life," Lydia Banks begged. "He's only 22. He can change. He's suffering. Our family are all suffering. . . . I'm just asking for you not to take his physical life!"

Lydia Banks ran out of the courtroom, weeping. Another sister, also hysterical, was ordered removed. Without the benefit or guidance of a professional evaluation, with no expert psychological testimony to assess, the jury sentenced Reid to die by lethal injection.

The problem is made worse by its unpredictability. "I always grant money for experts," says homicide judge David Savitt. But he admits that other judges routinely deny such requests. Because there is no institutional system governing either the request or the response, both the quality of defense and the outcome are widely divergent.

Some experts simply no longer provide their services to the defense. One psychiatrist who requested anonymity, and who, in the past, has testified for both prosecution and defense, now generally declines requests by defense attorneys to evaluate their clients. "Court-appointed lawyers are handcuffed," he says.

Dr. Robert Sadoff will no longer serve as an expert for the defense in court-appointed cases in Philadelphia—though he continues to testify in New Jersey, Ohio, Alabama, and Mississippi—because he cannot rely on promises of payment down the road. "I'm standing on the sidelines until a reliable and fair fee schedule, paid on time, is a regular part of the system," he says.

Former President Jimmy Carter once observed that

"life isn't fair." In the case of the death penalty, however, that unfairness can result in the execution of some for their inability to pay for the expert assistance many of us take for granted. "People with a lot of money are always going to get better services," says Judge Savitt. "But we aren't in the business of correcting every social problem."

The question is: Are we in the business of providing equal justice under law?

A Tale of Two Cities

In 1989, the Philadelphia courts—after an official request by the Philadelphia Bar Association—finally established new standards to qualify lawyers who would defend those charged with homicide. One new standard required that lawyers representing defendants facing the death penalty must have participated in at least one previous homicide trial. Another new qualification requires that homicide lawyers have participated in at least one death penalty training program within the past two years.

Norris Gelman, long recognized as one of the most effective capital defense lawyers in Philadelphia, says, "These standards are long overdue, but they come a little bit late for people that have already been poorly represented."

Tragically, such cases are not hard to find in Pennsylvania. In 1984, the Supreme Court of Pennsylvania upheld the death sentence of Richard Stoyko despite finding that "neither (appointed) trial counsel nor additional appointed counsel formally raised any issues regarding the penalty phase of the proceedings." It is during the penalty phase—following the jury's determination of guilt—that the jury hears evidence designed to guide it toward the appropriate penalty—life in prison or death. Without guidance, no jury can be expected to weigh this onerous choice fairly. It is a travesty of justice to ask this of a jury. Yet Stoyko's jury was asked to make precisely this determination.

As Associate Pennsylvania Supreme Court Justice Hutchinson noted in dissent, "The court-appointed counsel admitted . . . he had not read the United States Supreme Court's cases on capital punishment in preparation for this case and had never tried a homicide case. This coupled with the lack of any argument by anyone regarding the penalty phase, convinces me we have here . . . the absence of even minimally competent advocacy. . . . Ineffective assistance of counsel at the penalty phase of a capital case may be quite literally a matter of life and death."

The standards, though welcome innovations, are themselves seriously limited. In the words of one Philadelphia lawyer who participated in the development of the new standards, "They quantify. They do not qualify. They ask how many cases you've handled, not how well you handled them."

The Philadelphia District Attorney's office, which zealously prosecutes death penalty cases, insists on far more rigorous standards for its team of prosecutors than any imposed on defense attorneys. Every new recruit in the DA's office, for example, gets a three-week training course in general criminal law and Philadelphia procedures. Beyond that, according to the chief of homicide, Assistant District Attorney David Webb, to qualify for the homicide unit, an assistant DA must have at least five years as a prosecutor, with 25-30 major felony prosecutions.

Only after they have worked within the homicide unit for a year are they assigned their first capital case, and then as assisting counsel, or second chair, not as lead prosecutor. The goal is to recruit and train the best team of homicide prosecutors possible.

To seasoned capital defense attorney Norris Gelman, the difference is stark. "Their search for excellence is applauded," he notes. "Our search for bare competence is swept under the rug."

The difference between the Philadelphia experience and what occurs in Pittsburgh is also stark. The two Pennsylvania cities are similar in many respects—for instance, Philadelphia accounts for about 14 percent of the state's population, and Pittsburgh has about 12 percent. But whereas Philadelphia accounts for more than 50 percent of the population of Pennsylvania's death row, Pittsburgh accounts for less than 5 percent of death row inmates.

The difference can be attributed, at least in part, to a homicide defense team organized within the Pittsburgh Public Defender's office that has established ongoing litigation training and support. In hearings before the Judiciary Committee of the Commonwealth of Pennsylvania, Lester G. Nauhaus, Director of the Public Defender's Office of Allegheny County, testified: "Two lawyers always work on every capital case. . . . I am astounded that lawyers try capital cases in major metropolitan areas with only one attorney."

The Intractable Problem of Race

The appalling lack of legal and monetary resources accorded capital defendants in Philadelphia is exacerbated by other factors. Perhaps the most serious of these is one that plagues the application of the death penalty around the country: the destructive influence of race.

Many point to the record of Judge Sabo as an example of that influence. Sitting as a homicide judge from 1974 until his retirement in the early 1990s, he sentenced more people to death—26—than any judge in the state. When he retired, those sentences accounted for 40 percent of all those sentenced to death from Philadelphia, and thus more than 20 percent of all condemned prisoners in Pennsylvania. A whopping 24 of the 26 were black men.

One of those black men, who still remains on death row, is Mumia Abu-Jamal. Abu-Jamal was convicted of killing a police officer, although many people feel that he was unjustly accused. He was scheduled by Pennsylvania Governor Thomas Ridge to be executed by lethal injection on August 17, 1995. At the last minute he received a

145

temporary stay of the execution, which has now been postponed until after new evidence of his innocence can be evaluated.

Abu-Jamal was named Wesley Cook at birth in 1954 in a North Philadelphia housing project. In the tumultuous summer of 1968, the teenager and three friends attended a rally for presidential candidate George Wallace, shouting "Black Power!" while raising their fists to the air. Angry white Wallace supporters responded by beating him severely. When he yelled to a nearby police officer for help, that member of Philadelphia's finest kicked his face so brutally that his own mother did not recognize him in the hospital.

At 14, Abu-Jamal was already a radical, unquestionably fearless, and deeply opinionated. When he was 15 the FBI placed him under surveillance, and began amassing a file that eventually reached more than 700 pages. By 16 he was a founder of the Philadelphia branch of the Black Panther Party. In one of the police raids on Black Panther Party headquarters, Mumia recalls, an officer put a gun to his head and shouted, "Freeze, nigger. If you fucking blink, I'll blow your black goddam head off your shoulders."

After graduating from high school, Abu-Jamal studied politics at Goddard College in Vermont and then came back to Philadelphia to work at the student radio station at Temple University. By the 1970s he was a scrambling reporter working for several radio stations. He married and was often seen carrying his infant son with him on many assignments. He took on controversial subjects and became a minor celebrity around town.

In 1972, after an airplane flight to San Francisco, the FBI searched Abu-Jamal's luggage looking for weapons. The most threatening item they found after ripping his baggage apart was an X-Acto knife, the kind artists use for cutting paper. He was charged with possession of a dangerous weapon, although the absurd charges were soon dropped. But the FBI did not stop trying to incarcerate Abu-Jamal, who they considered to be a menacing revolutionary.

In 1981 Mumia was elected president of the Philadelphia chapter of the National Association of Black Journalists. He covered the growth of MOVE, a radical, back-to-nature black group that rejected elements of modern society, recycled refuse in their yards, and often allowed their children to run naked in their neighborhood. In response to citizen complaints, Philadelphia police began a siege of the area, cutting off food and supplies. The confrontation was quite similar to the 1993 siege of the Branch Davidian compound in Waco, Texas; both were escalating conflicts that erupted out of control. In Philadelphia, a gun battle ignited and one police officer was fatally wounded. In retaliation, Delbert Africa, a MOVE member and close friend of Mumia's, was beaten severely by the Philadelphia police—the event was captured on television cameras and in Abu-Jamal's mind forever. Nine MOVE members were charged with murder. Abu-Jamal became their champion, quitting his job at a National Public Radio station in a dispute over his coverage of MOVE.

About the same time that the Philadelphia police were harassing members of MOVE, they were being sued by the U.S. Department of Justice for widespread police brutality. The landmark lawsuit named Mayor Frank Rizzo, the police chief, and 18 senior police officers as defendants. This was the police department that ruled Philadelphia on December 9, 1981, when Abu-Jamal's life was turned upside down.

About 4 A.M. that morning, a young police officer, Daniel Faulkner, stopped a Volkswagen Beetle on a routine traffic violation. The driver of the car was Abu-Jamal's younger brother, who got into a dispute with Faulkner. While moonlighting as a cabdriver, Abu-Jamal saw his brother struggling with Faulkner. With his licensed .38 revolver in hand, Mumia came to his brother's aid. Backup police were called, and while Jamal's brother was placed under arrest, shots rang out. When the other officers arrived a few minutes later, two men were down—Faulkner dead from a gunshot wound, Abu-Jamal injured in the abdomen by a bullet from Faulkner's gun. Abu-Jamal filed a complaint against the police accusing the officers of beating him at the crime scene. The facts are in dispute, the police contending that Abu-Jamal fired first. Abu-Jamal contends that another man, seen running away from the incident by several eyewitnesses, shot Faulkner.

Abu-Jamal was tried for murder before Judge Sabo,

and was represented by a court-appointed attorney. The trial took place before Philadelphia's attorney guidelines were in place; even so, Abu-Jamal's lawyer admitted he was ill-prepared to handle the case. His admission was borne out by the fact that on several occasions, he missed chances to present important evidence that would vindicate his client. A jury of ten whites and two blacks took only four hours to find Abu-Jamal guilty and impose a death sentence. Whether Abu-Jamal killed officer Faulkner is subject to much debate. If he did so, it certainly was not premeditated—he did it either for self-defense or to protect his brother. In either event, Abu-Jamal's death sentence was not appropriate.

A more recent example of blatant racism came to light in July 1991, during a congressional hearing concerning the federal crime bill then being debated. In 1986, the Supreme Court held that systematic exclusion of blacks from juries violates the Constitution. However, the Court refused to apply the principle retroactively. An amendment to the crime bill under consideration at the hearing, the Berman Amendment, would have rectified this by permitting pre-1986 prisoners one year in which to raise claims that blacks had been unconstitutionally excluded from their juries.

The Philadelphia DA's office dispatched assistant district attorneys Gaele Barthold and Elizabeth Chambers to testify against the amendment. Committee Chairman Don Edwards asked, "Do you believe there is racism in the criminal justice system, especially in capital cases?"

Barthold replied, "I don't believe that this is something we see in Pennsylvania."

What both DAs had seen in Pennsylvania, however, was just such an unconstitutional, systematic exclusion of blacks by the head of the Philadelphia homicide unit, Assistant DA Barbara Christie. Indeed, Elizabeth Chambers, sitting next to Barthold at the hearing, had recently—and unsuccessfully—defended the practice before a federal magistrate.

Described by one defense attorney as "a vicious guided missile" whose prosecution tactics one homicide judge characterized as "outlandish" and "out of control," Christie had three times prosecuted accused murderer Charles Diggs. Three times she used her peremptory challenges to systematically exclude black jurors. In the second and third trials, she succeeded in seating all-white juries.

In March 1991, Federal Magistrate Richard Powers III recommended to the U.S. District Court that it grant *habeas corpus* relief in the case because Christie used all 15 of her discretionary strikes to seat an all-white jury, a practice prohibited by the Constitution. The magistrate wrote:

> Given the inescapable fact that members of the black race accounted for approximately one-third of Philadelphia's total population at the time of petitioner's trial, it is incredible that the assistant DA could not find one satisfactory black

150

juror capable of fairly sitting in judgment of the
petitioner.

Assistant DA [Christie] . . . kept a running
tabulation of the number of blacks left on the jury
after each challenge was exercised . . . a telling
indication of [her] predisposed prejudice toward
blacks on the jury . . . particularly when no white
jurors were challenged for any reasons whatsoever.
. . . The Assistant District Attorney testified that
she never used race as a factor to exclude a black
from a jury. . . . I find that . . . unworthy of belief.

On March 27, 1991, the U.S. District Court Chief
Judge, John P. Fullam, accepted the recommendation of
his magistrate, and granted the writ for *habeas corpus*.

When former Supreme Court Justice William Brennan
said of the death penalty, "It smacks of little more than a
lottery system," he might well have had Philadelphia in
mind. There, the poverty of individual defendants is
matched by the poverty of the city. This dual impover-
ishment starves the system of justice itself.

When you are poor in Philadelphia and charged with
a capital crime, one roll of the dice—the lawyer who will
represent you—goes a long way in determining your fate.

As unfair as this initial crapshoot may be, any
pretense to equal justice under law is fatally undermined
by the lack of available resources and their uneven distribution. When justice is defined differently for the poor

151

than for the rest of society, equal justice ceases to be a vaunted principle and becomes instead an empty slogan. In the realm of the death penalty, such inequality of application is intolerable to a just society. Like a house divided, justice divided cannot stand.

NO SUBSTITUTE FOR COMPETENCE

Sylvester Adams was executed in South Carolina in August 1995. He was a poor black man suffering from mental retardation and mental illness. His court-appointed lawyer failed to mention these crucial facts during the trial. Later, one of the jurors came forward and said that she would not have voted for the death penalty had she known Adams was retarded. The subsequent intervention of David Bruck, who represented Susan Smith at trial, and the South Carolina Resource Center, came too late. The hard reality is that there is simply no substitute for competent counsel at trial.

Judy Haney, an inmate on death row in Alabama, awaits her imminent execution largely because of incompetent counsel. Subjected to incessant beatings by her husband, Haney eventually struck back. She hired a man to kill her husband, a crime for which she was found guilty.

It is rare for a court to impose the death penalty on a woman who has asked another to murder her abusive spouse. Haney, however, had little assistance from her court-appointed lawyers. In fact, one of her attorneys could not find hospital records detailing the injuries Haney received from her husband, which would have reinforced her testimony about abuse. In addition, the trial had to be delayed for a day because the very same lawyer showed up for court too drunk to perform his job. He was held in contempt of court, and sent to jail overnight. A few days later, Haney was sentenced to death.

The evidence surrounding Haney's murder of her husband was not much different than the circumstances in other battered-wife cases. Yet Haney was sentenced to the electric chair, while others were not. Why? As in Philadelphia, the single biggest factor in determining whether a defendant will live or die is not the judge or the jury. Instead, the difference between life and death often is in the hands of court-appointed or volunteer attorneys, who are underpaid and frequently lacking proper qualifications. Without some way of assuring competent state-appointed counsel, the promise held out by the Supreme Court's decision in *Gideon* will remain largely unfulfilled.

In the era of media-enhanced courtroom spectacles, people have come to believe that all those accused of murder are entitled to and receive top-notch lawyers, a variety of experts, and fair judges. Yet the reality of America's capital punishment system differs greatly from the Simpson and Menendez theatrics. Ninety percent of those accused of murder cannot afford the team of experts that a wealthy defendant can call on. Indigent defendants are too poor to afford their own lawyer, and thus are assigned one by the government. Though the right to counsel is protected in the Constitution, the right to qualified and experienced counsel is not. Lawyers assigned to indigent defendants often lack the time and knowledge to try a capital case with any degree of competence.

The poor quality of assigned legal defense in murder cases leads to arbitrariness in the criminal justice system. While one defendant may have the good fortune to have his case taken by a large law firm or a well-equipped advocacy group such as the ACLU, another defendant accused of the same charges may be assigned a lawyer who has never tried a capital case and is being reimbursed for his efforts at a salary little better than minimum wage. In other words, the quality of government-assigned legal defense in this country is so varied that the right to counsel addressed in *Gideon* can lead to random and illogical sentencing.

In general, those who are on death row are those who cannot afford their own attorney, and studies have shown that the quality of the attorneys assigned to them is highly questionable. A six-month review by the *National Law Journal* of death penalty representation revealed that, especially in Southern states, where the majority of U.S. executions take place, there is a high disbarment rate for attorneys who have represented death row inmates, widespread inexperience among those appointed to capital cases, and a wholly unrealistic cap on the funds available to the defense. ("Fatal Defense," *National Law Journal*, June 11, 1990.)

*   *   *

For ten years, Federico Martinez Macias sat on death row in Texas, waiting to be executed for a murder which he claimed he did not commit. Macias was accused of slaying two people during a 1983 El Paso burglary. The state's case against Macias was weak at best—built on testimony from a man who had failed a polygraph test and was himself a suspect, and precious little hard evidence.

Yet Macias, like many of those accused of murder in the United States who cannot afford counsel, suffered because of his attorneys' incompetence. Underpaid and with little money to obtain expert witnesses and investigators, Macias's defense made repeated legal mistakes. One of the primary oversights involved the defense's failure to call an alibi witness who could have proved Macias was far away from where the murders took place, probably resulting in an acquittal. These sort of oversights are understandable, for over the eight-month period that he defended Macias, the lawyer was paid an average of $11.84 an hour. With that type of compensation, even the most qualified attorney would have a difficult time garnering the resources to challenge the prosecution's accusations.

Fortunately for Macias, his case was taken *pro bono* by the large, well-respected Washington, D.C., law firm of Skadden, Arps, Slate, Meagher and Flom in the post-conviction stage. One of the firm's partners, Douglas Robinson, took on the case and treated it as he would any of the other cases which his company handles. He and his assistants were more qualified to handle Macias's case, and had the added resources of time and money to devote to his plight. Initially, they spent tens of thousands of dollars, found a new eyewitness, and brought in the previously neglected alibi witness. Eventually, the Skadden group devoted $1 million worth of hours to the case, resulting in a 173-page petition urging the court to overturn Macias's conviction. The court reviewed the evidence and decided that Macias had indeed been deprived of adequate assistance of counsel, and granted him *habeas corpus*.

When a grand jury refused to reindict him, Macias was free at last. "I've had some of the worst representation and some of the best," Macias reflected. "Money makes a big difference." (Cohen, "The Difference a Million Makes," *Time*, June 19, 1995.)

Obviously, in order to avoid such inconsistencies in death penalty sentencing, it is necessary to improve the quality of the defense to which those accused of murder are entitled. However, despite the popular notion that our country is plagued by too many attorneys, there are actually too few attorneys accepting capital cases, and many of those that do accept are underqualified. The problem lies less in the abilities of the attorneys themselves than in the nature of state capital sentencing structure. Too often, county and state governments are unwilling to provide the necessary resources to assigned defense counsel. For some critical stages of appeal, defendants are given no attorney at all. Consequently, many of those accused do not receive a fair trial.

In most states which use the death penalty, the responsibility of providing an indigent with a lawyer falls to the county in which the case is to be tried. As counties vary widely in size and wealth, so does the compensation given court-appointed lawyers. In Texas, for instance, an attorney in Dallas or Houston might be paid at a rate that is close to what they might charge a private client, while in smaller counties attorneys may be paid as little as $10 an hour. In Kentucky, funding for a public defender case averaged $296.44 in one county, but only $44.22 in another. (Governor's Task Force on the Delivery and Funding of Quality Public Defender Service Interim Recommendations, reprinted in *Advocate*, December 1993.) Obviously, the defense attorney in the wealthier county can afford to hire more experts and do more research than can the attorney in the poorer county. In states like Alabama, Mississippi, and Louisiana, lawyers are sometimes working for about $5 an hour. (See "Fatal Defense.") Often times a public defender is given only $800 for an entire case, barely enough to cover overhead and surely not enough to obtain the usual experts and research necessary to try a capital case.

The rate of compensation often determines the quality of representation. Local judges usually determine at the beginning of a trial the fee that will be paid the defense attorney. This figure can be set intentionally low, purposefully hindering the defense's efforts to represent the accused. The prosecution, on the other hand, can call on a team of salaried state employees with ample resources and ready access to other law enforcement agencies for investigating and pursuing their cases. Without adequate compensation, a thorough defense that could even begin to challenge the capacities of the prosecution is out of the question.

Some might argue that lawyers should have an ethical obligation to represent indigent defendants, but this ignores the reality of maintaining a legal practice. Due to the time that must be devoted to something as complicated as a capital case, some lawyers have to practically shut down the rest of their practices. They simply do not have the time or money to pursue anything else. In addition, many capital trials by the nature of the crime committed prove highly unattractive. A lawyer assigned to represent a defendant accused of murder may feel pressure from those in the community in which the murder was committed. Because of public outrage and cries for the death penalty, many lawyers try to avoid these cases, and if assigned to defend such an unattractive client, may make little attempt to get the client off lest they leave themselves open to the wrath of an enraged community.

LET SLEEPING ATTORNEYS LIE

In other cases, assigned counsel may give little or no effort because they feel the case is a lost cause or simply a burden and a waste of time. The August 14, 1992 *Houston Chronicle* headline, for example, read "John Makeig, Asleep on the Job; Slaying Trial Boring, Lawyer Said." The assigned defense attorney for a man facing death dozed during portions of the trial. When the defendant questioned the judge as to whether his lawyer's behavior was tolerable in a courtroom, the judge replied, "The Constitution does not say that the lawyer has to be awake." Not surprisingly, given such poor representation and the lack of sympathy from the bench, the defendant was sentenced to death.

Often, especially in some Southern states which are notorious for sending defendants to death row, racism is a prevalent factor amongst the defense attorneys. In one Texas case, the attorney for the defense referred to his client as a "wetback" in front of an all-white jury. (*Ex parte Guzmon*, 730 S.W. 2d 724, 736; Texas Criminal Appeals 1987.) In a case in Georgia, the only reference that an appointed attorney made to his client consisted of the following: "You have got a little old nigger man over there that doesn't weigh over 135 pounds. He is poor and he is broke. He's got an appointed lawyer. . . . He is ignorant. I will venture to say he has an IQ of not over 80." (Transcript of Opening and Closing Arguments at 39, *State v. Dungee*, Record of Excerpts at 102, 11th Circuit, No. 85-8202., decided sub. nom.) Needless to say, the defendant was sentenced to death. The lawyer, however, was just perceptive enough in observing that his client was "ignorant." In fact, had he done even a cursory check into his client's background, he would have discovered that the man was mentally retarded and was unable to perform many basic tasks. (*Dungee v. State*, No. 444 [Superior Court Seminole County, Georgia], on change of venue, No. 887CR-53445 [Superior Court Muscogee County, Georgia 1988].)

In another Georgia case, a man named John Young received a death sentence after being defended by an attorney who was addicted to drugs and who had emotional and physical problems which impeded his ability to concentrate on the trial. (Affidavit of Charles Marchman, Jr. at 1-5, 7, *Young v. Kemp*, No. 885-98-2-MAC [M.D. Georgia 1985].) Less than a month after the trial Young again encountered his lawyer—this time behind bars at the county prison. The attorney had been sent to jail on state and federal drug charges. John Young was later executed by the state of Georgia.

Given these examples of legal malpractice, it seems amazing that attorneys such as these get assigned to such important work as capital cases. However, a look at who chooses the attorneys is instructive. On the county level, judges choose representation for indigents and set fees for cases. Many of these judges are former prosecutors who have been elected by the community in which they live and practice law. Because of their obligations to those who are responsible for their position, many judges feel a responsibility to ensure that murderers are punished swiftly and harshly. Many times this carries over into their appointment of counsel.

By assigning attorneys who have never tried capital cases and providing them with little compensation, these judges stack the odds against defendants. In one Florida case, the judge had to call the defense attorney into his chambers to explain to him the proceedings in a capital trial. "I'm at a loss," the lawyer claimed. "I really don't know what to do in this type of proceeding. If I'd been through one I would, but I've never handled one except this time." (*Douglas v. Wainwright*, 714 F.2d 1532, 1556 [11th Circuit 1983], vacated and remanded.) Because the assigned counsel often has little experience and few resources to rely on, the judge need do no more than sit back and let the case decide itself, freeing himself from any accountability for the final sentence. In addition, judges do not request the assistance of the top lawyers in the region, who they think have more important and more financially rewarding cases on which to work.

Nobody seems willing to call this practice of appointing inexperienced, unqualified counsel into question. Those who receive shoddy legal defense, although constitutionally entitled to a fair trial, are normally those most scorned by society—poor and with little power to change the system. Those with the power to change the system, namely the courts and legislatures, refrain from doing so because the current system empowers them.

Thus, nobody speaks out when an assigned defense attorney fails to raise even the most basic protections allowed in the Bill of Rights. One poor Jefferson County, Georgia man accused of murder loudly protested the lawyer assigned to him by the court—apparently with good reason. The lawyer neglected to uphold his client's right to a representative jury chosen without racial discrimination. The population of Jefferson County was over 50 percent African American, yet the trial jury, which eventually sentenced the defendant to death, was only 20 percent African American. The lawyer's ignorance was incredible: when later questioned about any criminal cases with which he was familiar, he could come up with only two—Miranda and Dred Scott. Dred Scott was not a criminal case. (Transcript of hearing of April 25-27, 1988, at 231, *State v. Birt* [Superior Court Jefferson County, Georgia 1988] No. 2360.)

Assigned counsel may neglect to provide a defendant with all the rights he is entitled to during trial and sentencing. The accused's situation worsens after he has been sentenced to death. The Constitution does not necessarily require that all defendants be provided counsel *after* conviction. Although a death row defendant might hope to demonstrate how his attorney's poor performance resulted in his conviction and sentence, he generally cannot afford an attorney, and more often than not has not appealed the initial verdict.

Because the current process of assigning counsel in capital cases favors the prosecutors and the judges, state governments have little reason to change the structure. By championing the death sentence and the processes that

162

produce larger death row populations, those in government take on an appearance of political toughness in their constituent's eyes. Any call to raise the fees paid assigned counsel or to increase the legal resources available to those accused of capital crimes goes unheeded while legislators hide behind the mask of being "tough on crime."

PROVIDING HOPE: OHIO'S RULE 65

Despite the apparently bleak situation for indigent defendants, there are some common-sense, cost-efficient solutions to the problems that they face. In Ohio, Rule 65 was adopted in 1987 by the Ohio Supreme Court to help change the situation in which "inexperienced and under-compensated attorneys often were not providing effective representation in capital cases." (Second Report of the Committee on the Appointment of Counsel for Indigent Defendants in Capital Cases, Judge Everett Burton, Chair, April 1993.) Ohio was the first state to set mandatory standards for the quality of appointed counsel in capital cases.

Rule 65 states that only experienced and qualified lawyers can be eligible to defend indigent defendants. In addition, courts need to assign two lawyers, ensuring further competence and attention in representation. Because capital cases are so complex and time-consuming, a single assigned counsel often cannot give adequate representation. Indeed, in Texas, which executes more people than any other state, defendants are often assigned only one attorney. In Philadelphia, where the Abu-Jamal case has highlighted the deficiencies of death penalty sentencing, and where more people are sentenced to death each year than the combined death rows of 21 states which use the death penalty, single defense attorneys are often the norm. (Hines, "Circumstances in Philadelphia Consign Killers," *New York Times*, June 8, 1992.)

Rule 65 also specifies that assigned attorneys are required to attend 12 hours of specialized training every two years, and must have adequate experience in the trials of other serious felonies as well. To ensure that the quality of counsel remains high throughout the state, the court responsible for assigning counsel must monitor the attorney's performance during trial. If, as in the case of John Young, the lawyer performs at such a level that the defendant does not receive adequate representation, that lawyer can then be banned from accepting any more capital cases.

One of the essential solutions to the problem of poor indigent representation is the establishment of statewide bodies to set standards for capital representation and the creation in each state of a division of full-time, salaried, qualified attorneys for all stages of a capital case. Such groups would require adequate and consistent compensation levels to be established throughout each state to ensure an even quality of representation. If the level of defense competence rises, as studies and practical experience indicates, there will certainly be fewer people sentenced to death row. Because defense attorney errors are often the grounds for appeal in capital cases, the quantity of appeals will most certainly shrink.

Yet with many politicians calling for expansion of the death penalty to crimes other than murder, and states such as New York bringing back capital punishment, the inconsistencies and injustices occurring now in places like Pennsylvania, Texas, and Georgia will surely occur even more frequently. While judges and juries seem inclined to sentence defendant after defendent to death row, few acknowledge the consequences for our basic democratic concepts of justice of a growing death row population that our public defender system cannot serve. The crisis in death penalty representation that stems from lack of funds and political will augurs poorly for the country as a whole. Unless we turn back the rush to vengeance and start to limit the use of the death penalty, this national problem will only escalate.

8

THOU SHALT NOT KILL
BIBLICAL, THEOLOGICAL, AND MORAL
DIMENSIONS OF THE DEATH PENALTY

Father, forgive them for they know not what they do.
—Jesus Christ,
      while dying on the cross

Vanity asks the question, "Is it popular?" Politics
asks the question, "Is it expedient?" Religion asks
the question, "Is it right?" At the core of every
political, economic, or social issue are religious, moral,
and spiritual dimensions.

We are all spiritual, moral, social, economic, and political beings, whether or not we are aware of each dimension and how they interact. The ideal is to be conscious of
and develop each and every dimension to its fullest capac-
ity while maintaining a balance with the others.

While we are all equal before God, and should be equal before the law, our finitude—and, from a Christian perspective, our sin—prevents us from achieving this ideal. Precisely because life is not an ideal, but real, we are forced to make imperfect choices in an imperfect world.

The spiritual and the temporal, the sacred and the secular, are intertwined. By denying their interrelatedness, the left and the right—religiously and politically— are allied in a way that they seldom recognize. Conservative religious people, who sometimes argues that they are not, or should not, be involved in politics, proclaim that they are keeping their eyes on heaven and heavenly things—unconsciously blessing the status quo, whether just or unjust, and never offering political leaders moral or ethical challenges. They may offer complaints, but since the political realm is none of their real business, they never put forth a moral challenge.

The political left, which sometimes reduces life to the material and secular dimensions, dismisses the moral, religious, and spiritual dimensions as unreal or unnecessary. Thus, it is left only with economic and political power with which to achieve its lofty ideals and goals.

Therefore, both religious right and political left agree, after a fashion, that politics and religion have nothing to do with each other. The former lives in the world of the *ought* (how things ought to be), disconnected from the *is* (the real world); while the latter lives in the world of the *is*, disconnected from the *ought*. The traditional Judeo-Christian view obligates the oughtness of life to confront

167

the isness of life, compelling the isness of life to wrestle with the oughtness of life. While we must make decisions and act, a certain humility born of ambiguity and less-than-absolute certainty is often characteristic of those who see life and its choices and complexities through a glass darkly.

When Jesus said, "Render therefore unto Caesar the things that are Caesar's; and unto God the things that are God's" (Matthew 22:21), he was saying and confirming that God is, government is, and each has its proper place. He was saying, I'll share with you some principles and the spirit with which to confront the world, but the circumstances of life are too intricate for me to give you a formula for every situation. Using your gifts of mind and spirit, and with God's help, do the best you can to answer the questions and deal with the issues as they arise. The constant struggle is to understand what *is*, and how the things that are Caesar's and the things that are God's interrelate and coexist with each other.

In terms of motivation, my politics do not make me religious—my religion makes me political. The Bible's directive to feed the hungry leads me in a direct line from the hungry person to my own pantry to the soup line to the Agriculture Department to national and international agriculture policies. My religious beliefs inform my political beliefs. I implement my religious goals through a concrete political system.

Likewise, the issue of civil order leads me from those individuals who create civil disorder (criminals) to the means and issues involved in protecting civil order (jails and/or capital punishment), which is the judicial system.

An elementary lesson of both education and television is that nothing teaches like a concrete example. Philosophy and abstract concepts contribute little to mass education. Identify a concrete real-life example, effectively tell that story, and people will identify with it and learn.

It was in that context that on July 25, 1995, I decided to write a personal letter, to be shared openly with the broader community, to the Rev. A. L. Brackett, the African American pastor of St. Paul Baptist Church, and the Rev. Dr. Thomas Currie, the white pastor of the First Presbyterian Church, both of Union, South Carolina. I had worked and was impressed with both of them in a previous visit to Union.

I wrote this letter in the midst of the sentencing hearing for Susan Smith, the woman who was convicted of killing her two small sons by locking them in a car and then driving the car into a lake near Union. It was an awful, almost unbelievable crime. At first, Smith tried to pass the blame by claiming that a black man had kidnapped her children, but when diligent work by the police brought the investigation around to her, she confessed to having killed them herself. During and after her trial, there were many, many people who wanted to see her sentenced to death.

The letter I sent to the two pastors counseled against the ultimate punishment for Susan Smith:

169

Dear Rev. Brackett & Rev. Dr. Currie:

Today I write to you as a way of writing to other ministers, churches, and members of the faith community in South Carolina regarding Susan Smith. I appeal to those of you within the faith community, and I appeal through you to those of humane concern and moral conscience outside the faith community, to spare the life of Susan Smith. We must join hands and hearts and pray that her life be spared.

In a state of sickness, bewilderment, and passion, Susan Smith did indeed kill her two babies in a horrendous crime. In addition, she tried a clever act, accusing a black man of doing it, which, for a few days, compounded the crisis, and could have led to a massive escalation of the crisis. Fortunately, the law enforcement officials involved were professional, disciplined, and skilled enough to discover the truth through a thorough investigation and avert an even worse situation.

I want to make a moral, religious, and humane appeal for the life of Susan Smith. Killing another human being anywhere—whether in Bosnia, the Middle East, South Africa, or Union, South Carolina—diminishes human life everywhere, whatever the format of death.

First, killing Susan Smith through capital punishment will not bring her two boys back.

170

They have gone to be with God. They are at peace in heaven.

Second, the math does not add up. The state's killing of Susan Smith would not subtract from, negate, or cancel the tragedy; it would only multiply death and add hurt, injury, and pain to more people. It would add pain and suffering to more families and leave even more people in distress and grieving.

The feelings of anger and anguish of those who knew and loved these two precious little boys is understandable, legitimate, and real. For precisely those reasons, however, the state should be in the position of breaking the cycle of violence, not perpetuating it.

Third, capital punishment was not a deterrent for her and it will not be a deterrent for others. It was a crime committed by a weak, troubled, and confused woman. Even though I am universally opposed to capital punishment as a matter of principle, in her case she was not even a vicious gangster who conspired to kill someone for financial gain. She was not out to destroy our government, as those who blew up the federal building in Oklahoma City apparently were. She was not dealing in dope at someone else's expense. She was simply a sick young woman who killed in a moment of passion.

Fourth, if protecting society is the issue, then

171

life in jail without the possibility of parole will protect society and deter her from committing any further crimes. [I later found out, according to South Carolina law, that "life" but not "life without parole" was the only legal option.]

Fifth, if punishment is the issue, she will be in mental agony for the rest of her life—a living hell on earth of memories of her innocent children.

Sixth, the only real reason for killing Susan Smith is vengeance. Yet my Bible tells me, "Vengeance is mine saith the Lord." Vengeance from men and women begets retaliation and more vengeance. What are we teaching our children if we kill her? We are teaching them the ethic of street gangs, an eye for an eye and a tooth for a tooth. If we use that approach, we will all end up blind and disfigured. As Ghandi said, "An eye for an eye makes the whole world blind."

What would Jesus do? He was a victim of capital punishment at the hands of the state. He said, as he hung on the cross, "Father, forgive them for they know not what they do." Capital punishment implicates the state in deliberate, systematic, vengeful violence. What would Jesus say? Would Jesus pull the switch or administer the lethal injection? I don't think so on the basis of what he taught. He taught, "Blessed are the merciful, for they shall obtain mercy."

When the state engages in capital punishment,

it assumes a God-like posture, and again my Bible tells me that "You shall have no other gods before me." When the state engages in capital punishment, it takes away that which it does not have the power to give—life itself—and, while not an issue in the case of Susan Smith, if in the future a mistake is made and an innocent person is put to death, that life can never be given back. Only God should have the power to give and take life, and that in due season and according to His own plan.

Mercy lifts us all. Death lowers us all. Mercy is the only way to escape the cycle of violence. South Carolina could lead the way in mercy and in breaking the cycle of death, if it spares the life of Susan Smith.

Again, my Bible tells me another story of a woman who was condemned to capital punishment for committing a sin. Jesus came upon her and saw what was happening. He asked the men who were preparing to stone her to death, "Let him among you who is without sin cast the first stone." One by one they dropped their rocks and went away. He told the woman, "They do not condemn you and neither do I. Go, and sin no more."

Susan Smith did more than commit a sin, she committed a dreadful act—the crime of murder. Justice would not be served by merely condemning her, but neither is justice served by killing her. In this instance, justice is best served when tempered with the mercy of life in prison without possibility of parole.

The Susan Smith test gives us another opportunity to rise above the walls of race and gender that separate us and seek the common ground of justice tempered with grace and mercy. We will all be better people if we do. Pain abounds, but moral power must abound even more. Our spiritual challenge is to turn our human pain into God's moral power. Moral power is the power to save, and the power to save is the power we seek.

In Christian Love,

Reverend Jesse L. Jackson

I hope—I *believe*—that this letter reached some people and changed their attitudes.

OFFICIAL CHURCH POLICIES

While many religious figures have opposed the death penalty for hundreds of years, organized religion was slow to do so as official policy. The first mainline church body to go on record against the death penalty was the Methodist Church in 1956. In a resolution, the church stated, "We deplore the use of capital punishment." The United Methodist Church has reaffirmed the anti-death penalty statement every four years.

The United Church of Canada (1956), the American

Baptists (1958), the Union of American Hebrew Congregations (1959), and the American Ethical Union (1960) soon joined with statements of moral opposition to capital punishment.

A few other mainline church voices were added to the opposition in the 1960s: the United Church of Christ (1962), the Reformed Church (1965), the Presbyterian Church (1965-1966), and the Lutheran Church (1966) each passed resolutions opposing the death penalty. Toward the end of the decade, the National Council of Churches was finally able to assemble enough votes from its member churches to go on record against capital punishment.

Between 1930 and 1964, 54.7 percent of all executed prisoners in the U.S. were people of color. It therefore makes sense that the public debate over capital punishment during the period of the late 1950s and 1960s coincided with the modern civil rights movement. The rising consciousness of civil rights (and wrongs) helped to set a climate which led to a decline in the use of the death penalty, even though it was still legal in most states. During the 1950s, there was an average of 70 or more executions in the United States annually, down from an average of more than 120 in the 1940s. Beginning in 1960, the number of executions dropped steadily, from 56 to 2 in 1967.

The 1967 executions were the last ones for a number of years. This informal moratorium on capital punishment took place because states were waiting for the Supreme Court to decide whether the death penalty

175

violated the Fourteenth Amendment principle of equal protection as a result of the large number of African Americans and poor people who were sentenced to death; also whether it constituted cruel and unusual punishment and thus was in violation of the Eighth Amendment.

In 1972, in a victory for the foes of the death penalty, the Supreme Court ruled that all state capital punishment laws, as they currently existed, were unconstitutional. However, the Court also ruled that the states could rewrite their death penalty laws to fall within constitutional limits. Thus, within a short period of time after the ruling, 35 states had reinstated their capital punishment laws, changing them in an attempt to comply with the Supreme Court's ruling.

But this triggered still another debate, this time joined by the Roman Catholic Church in the United States. In 1974, through its bishops, the church issued a brief, but decisive, statement: "The U.S. Catholic Conference goes on record in opposition to capital punishment."

Additionally, U.S. Roman Catholic bishops urged the following goals for public policy:

A national commitment to economic and social justice and the elimination of poverty and of racism as an effective means of reducing crime. This policy should include programs to involve citizens, neighborhoods, and organizations in preventing crime and in monitoring the criminal justice system, especially aimed at humanizing the

176

penal system; knowledge of the rights of the accused, adequate legal representation, representative juries, competent judges, speedy trials, due process, and judicial integrity; just compensation of victims of crime; abolition of capital punishment; development of alternatives to prisons, rehabilitative services, and reintegration of offenders into the community.

The more conservative churches fought back. The National Association of Evangelicals (1972), the Lutheran Church-Missouri Synod (1976), and the National Association of Free Will Baptists (1977) all passed resolutions favoring capital punishment. The 16-million-member Southern Baptist Convention has not spoken on the issue.

The next tactic for those opposed to capital punishment was to try to prevent the enforcement of the death penalty. That failed when, on January 17, 1977, Gary Gilmore was put to death in Utah. Five more on death row were executed over the next five years. Twenty-one were executed in 1984. The number of executions, as well as the number of people sitting on death row, has continued to grow.

The tactics now among most religious opponents has shifted back to limiting the number of crimes for which the punishment of death can be applied, to conducting prison ministries, and to reforming the criminal justice system generally. Congress, however, currently seems to be legislating in the opposite direction.

There has been a slow, but steady, growth of opposition to the death penalty within the formal structures of many religious bodies. A large challenge still remains, however, to convince church members and the general public of the moral, social, and economic bankruptcy of continuing to pursue a death penalty policy.

THE BIBLE AND THE DEATH PENALTY

For Jews the Old Testament, and for Christians the entire Bible, but especially the New Testament, is the final authority for their faith and practice.

For some, quoting the Bible to support one's position is a little like what they say about those who use statistics—i.e., statistics do not lie, but liars use statistics. Both religionists who support and religionists who oppose capital punishment try to show that the Bible supports them. In theological circles this is known as "proof texting": finding a biblical text that "proves" your point, rather than explaining the text in context, then applying that central truth to a current situation.

Without being absolutist, I think it can be fairly stated that religious conservatives, who often read the Bible in more literal terms, use various scriptures to support their position in support of capital punishment. Religious liberals, on the other hand, who tend to see the Bible in less literal terms, try to divine in scripture general

178

principles and a spirit that combines the demands of justice tempered with mercy and grace. The two camps even cite some of the same verses as their opponents.

I think religious liberals, more than religious conservatives, tend to accept and utilize modern biblical studies, exegesis, and interpretation, and also tend to be more open to the development of the social and psychological sciences, including studies in crime and penology, more than their conservative religious friends.

The Old Testament gives rather explicit support to capital punishment. Many scriptures can be cited to boost the religious belief that capital punishment is demanded, sanctioned by, or is at least acceptable to God. Oft-quoted scriptures to sustain this point include the following:

EXODUS 21:12-17: Anyone who strikes a man and so causes his death, must die. If he has not lain in wait for him but God has delivered him into his hands, then I will appoint you a place where he may seek refuge. But should a man dare to kill his fellow by treacherous intent, you must take him even from my altar to be put to death. Anyone who abducts a man—whether he has sold him or is found in possession of him—must die. Anyone who curses father or mother must die.

EXODUS 21:23-25: . . . but should she die, you shall give life for life, eye for eye, tooth for tooth, hand for hand, foot for foot, burn for burn, wound for wound, stroke for stroke.

This is known as the law of *lex talionis*, or "an eye for an eye and a tooth for a tooth." This is usually misunderstood and interpreted as vengeful. However, that was not its intent. Its real intent was to set limits—to make sure that the payment did not exceed the debt actually incurred.

EXODUS 21:28-29: When an ox gores a man or woman to death, the ox must be stoned. Its flesh shall not be eaten, and the owner of the ox shall not be liable. But if the ox has been in the habit of goring before, and if its owner was warned but has not kept it under control, then should this ox kill a man or woman, the ox must be stoned and its owner put to death.

EXODUS 22:18: Anyone who has intercourse with an animal must die.

LEVITICUS 20:2: Tell the sons of Israel: Any son of Israel or any stranger living in Israel must die if he hands over any of his children to Molech.

LEVITICUS 20:10-16: The man who commits adultery with a married woman; The man who commits adultery with his neighbor's wife must die, he and his accomplice. The man who lies with his father's wife has uncovered his father's nakedness. Both of them must die, their blood shall be on their own heads. The man who lies with his daughter-in-law; both of them must die;

they have defiled each other, their blood shall be on their own heads.

LEVITICUS 20:27: Any man or woman who is a necromancer or magician must be put to death by stoning; their blood shall be on their own heads.

From these brief readings, one can see that capital punishment was permitted for about a dozen offenses in ancient Hebrew law, including, but not limited to, murder, kidnapping, selling a person into slavery, adultery, incest, bestiality, and witchcraft. During war, even more drastic measures were permitted against a defeated enemy. The primary method was stoning, but burning, beheading, and the use of a sword or spear were also practiced.

While most religious conservatives would not argue that we should apply the death penalty to all of the "crimes" cited in the Old Testament, most would argue that the scriptures do permit, and God does sanction, capital punishment for certain heinous crimes.

While the New Testament says nothing directly about capital punishment, there are those who argue that there are scriptures that indirectly support capital punishment. One of the most often cited is from Paul's writings, Romans 13:1-3:

Let every soul be subject unto the higher powers. For there is no power but of God, the powers that be are ordained of God. Whosoever therefore resisteth the power, resisteth the ordinance of God; and they shall receive unto themselves damnation. For the rulers are not a terror to good works, but to the evil.

This scripture is used to legitimize civil governments, including justifying their various functions, such as taxing the people to support government programs, serving in the military to defend the country, and capital punishment to deter crime and protect society.

Supporters of the death penalty also cite the fact that when Jesus was tried and sentenced to die, and even when he was actually on the cross, he never once protested or challenged the government's authority to practice capital punishment.

Opponents of the death penalty cite the lack of any justification of the capital punishment or a defense of it in the New Testament. Their logic seems to be this: if the New Testament does not mandate it, then it should not be practiced. Opponents often use the following verses to shore up their position:

MATTHEW 22:17-21: Tell us your opinion, then. Is it permissible to pay taxes to Caesar or not? But Jesus was aware of their malice and replied, You hypocrites! Why do you set this trap for me? Let me see the money you pay the tax with. They handed him a denarius, and he said, Whose head is this? Whose name? Caesar's they replied. He then said to them, Very well, give

182

back to Caesar what belongs to Caesar—and to God what belongs to God.

MATTHEW 5:25-26: Come to terms with your opponent in good time while you are still on the way to the court with him, or he may hand you over to the judge and the judge to the officer, and you will be thrown into prison. I tell you solemnly, you will not get out till you have paid the last penny.

I PETER 2:13-14: For the sake of the Lord, accept the authority of every social institution; the emperor, as the supreme authority, and the governors as commissioned by him to punish criminals and praise good citizenship.

ACTS 5:29-30: In reply Peter and the apostles said, Obedience to God comes before obedience to men; it was the God of our ancestors who raised up Jesus, but it was you who had him executed by hanging on a tree.

TITUS 3:1: Remind them that it is their duty to be obedient to the officials and representatives of the government.

ROMANS 13:3-4: Good behavior is not afraid of magistrates; only criminals have anything to fear. If you want to live without being afraid of authority, you must live honestly and authority may even honor you.

ROMANS 13:6-7: This is also the reason why you must pay taxes, since all government officials are God's officers. They serve God by collecting taxes. Pay every government officials what he has a right to ask—whether it be direct tax or indirect, fear or honor.

And of course, JOHN 8:3-11: The scribes and Pharisees brought a woman along who had been caught committing adultery; and making her stand there in full view of everybody, they said to Jesus, Master, this woman was caught in the very act of committing adultery, and Moses has ordered us in the Law to condemn women like this to death by stoning. What have you to say? They asked him this as a test, looking for something to use against him. But Jesus bent down and started writing on the ground with his finger. As they persisted with their question, he looked up and said, If there is one of you who has not sinned, let him be the first to thrown a stone at her. Then he bent down and wrote on the ground again. When they heard this they went away one by one, beginning with the eldest, until Jesus was left alone with the woman, who remained standing there. He looked up and said, Woman, where are they? Has no one condemned you? No one, sir, she replied. Neither do I condemn you, said Jesus. Go away, and don't sin any more.

Generally speaking, opponents of capital punishment ignore and/or dismiss the Old Testament writings in defense of capital punishment as not pertinent in the modern world; just as supporters of capital punishment dismiss many of the "sins" for which these Old Testament scriptures say capital punishment should be applied.

While everyone may have a view and an opinion, not all views and opinions are equal. While everyone may have a conscience, not everyone has an informed conscience. The views and opinions of trained experts, those with knowledge and/or experience in a given field, and those with disciplined minds and developed moral sensitivities, while not always right, should be listened to carefully and their input taken seriously. While I oppose the death penalty, I respect the right to disagree and respect those who have seriously wrestled with the issue of capital punishment and have come to a different conclusion.

THE FIFTH COMMANDMENT

The Fifth Commandment, of course, is "Thou shalt not kill." Read literally, that should theologically settle the question of the justness of the death penalty. It does not.

Historically, there have been three types of killing acceptable by the church and its theologians: killing in the context of conducting a "just war"; killing in self-defense; and killing in the form of capital punishment to protect society. Here I shall deal only with the third type.

Whatever the human, humane, or societal objections to capital punishment may be, the Judeo-Christian opposition begins with the premise that God is the creator and human beings are the creatures. From this religious viewpoint, life is not accidental; it is providential. Life is sacred. Therefore, other human beings do not have the right, and should not be given the power, to take away what God has created.

Psalms 8:3-5 says:

I look up at your heavens, made by your fingers,
at the moon and stars you set in place—
ah, what is man that you should spare a thought
    for him,
the son of man that you should care for him?

Yet you have made him little less than a god (or
    the angels)
you have crowned him with glory and splendor

If God created each human being a "little less than the angels," then all life—even the life of a guilty criminal, one who did not treat other lives as sacred, a human being who has gone astray—is sacred, must be revered, and must be treated with dignity and respect. Even the criminal has certain God-given human rights—the right to a fair judicial process, and to fair and humane punishment that fits the crime.

That does not mean that the rights or the plight of the victims of crime are not protected, preserved, and honored. It simply means that the rights and the dignity of all human beings—victims and victimizers—must be respected and protected. It is understandable that the victims of crime (and their families and loved ones) might not feel this way. That is why a dispassionate and just society, and the law, must preserve the rights and dignity of all concerned.

God is just, and does not object to a society protecting itself with the law by preventing further crime and punishing criminals who violate other human beings and break the law. But from a Judeo-Christian perspective, appropriate punishment must answer several questions and pass several tests.

First, what is the *purpose* of the punishment? Its purpose must be twofold: to reform the individual and to achieve retribution—to make the person pay a just price for the crime. Obviously, capital punishment eliminates the first, for a dead person cannot be reformed or rehabilitated. The second raises the question of proportionality, or fitting the punishment to the crime: Are the means limited to achieving the just end? Are the means in proportion to the just end?

Second, what are the *motives* of those doing the punishing? From a Judeo-Christian perspective, vindictive and vengeful motives are unacceptable: "Vengeance is mine saith the Lord." If the motive of punishment is pure, then a person who committed a crime because he were mentally or emotionally sick or socially scarred would be incarcerated, treated, and rehabilitated, not executed. If he were fully responsible for the crime, he would be incarcerated—

187

punished in proportion to the crime—and rehabilitated (if possible), not executed. If rehabilitation were impossible, and a judgment is made that the criminal is incapable of self-restraint and would commit further crimes and would further endanger other citizens and society, then life in prison without chance of parole would both prevent further crime and protect society.

Third, how *effective* is the punishment? Some state that capital punishment is the lesser of two evils—that the state must kill certain criminals in order to safeguard society by deterring other individuals from committing the same crimes. If that is the argument, then the burden of proof falls on those who support it to show conclusive proof that the death penalty not only deters crime, but that it is a necessary deterrent. As Chapter 6 indicated, some research suggests that use of the death penalty may actually increase violence in society while other research suggests that it makes no difference, but there is no valid evidence indicating that capital punishment is a deterrent.

Fourth, in a slightly broader dimension, is the question of *due respect* for the decent opinion of mankind. World opinion is increasingly against capital punishment. More and more governments are outlawing its use. The United States is aligned with the so-called "rogue" states of the world who continue to use the death penalty, and is one of only six nations that executes minors. The rest of the Judeo-Christian world is moving away from capital punishment as a way of dealing with crime and criminality. It would be well for our souls if we joined them.

188

9

FAITH, POPULAR OPINION, AND THE FUTURE OF CAPITAL PUNISHMENT

The late Supreme Court Justice Thurgood Marshall had great faith in the intelligence and morality of the American people. He believed that if we had the facts about capital punishment, we would find it shockingly immoral and absolutely unsupportable. If only the general public knew that the death penalty was no better a deterrent than life imprisonment; that very few convicted murderers actually receive the death penalty; that those who do are disproportionately poor and black; that carrying out an execution, with its lengthy appeals process, costs taxpayers more than life imprisonment; then the American people would certainly choose to abolish the use of capital punishment.

Although in *Furman v. Georgia* the Court did not rule on the constitutionality of the death penalty itself, but only on how it was applied, Justice Marshall expressed his faith in the people in his opinion on the case:

> I cannot believe that at this stage in our history, the American people would ever knowingly support purposeless vengeance. Thus, I believe that the great mass of citizens would conclude . . . that the death penalty is immoral and therefore unconstitutional.

Given the overwhelming evidence that the death penalty served no purpose except as a symbol of public wrath and vengeance and his conviction that an informed public would find the death penalty insupportable, Marshall stated unequivocally that the death penalty was unconstitutional. He was the only one of the nine justices to state this.

Unfortunately, neither the Court nor many other branches of government ever responded to Marshall's call for informed public opinion about the death penalty. Instead of testing true popular opinion, in deciding *Gregg v. Georgia*, the case that reinstated the death penalty, the Court looked to the number of state legislatures that had enacted new death penalty statutes and relatively restrictive Gallup polls as the expression of public sentiment regarding capital punishment.

The question we need to consider is whether

Thurgood Marshall was right. Do we, as a nation and as a people, deserve the faith he placed in us? How does America really feel about the death penalty? Would an America that understood the injustices of the death penalty firmly and righteously disavow it? Or was Justice Marshall poignantly naive about the true character of the bloodthirsty American people?

Determining what the American public really believes about capital punishment is not a frivolous undertaking with merely academic effects. In *Gregg* and in other cases, what the Court believed was the will of the people was a determining factor in reinstating the death penalty. Capital punishment will never be eliminated without an even more dramatic outpouring of public opinion against its use.

TESTING THE MARSHALL HYPOTHESIS

Justice Marshall's absolute belief that the dissemination of information containing the real facts about capital punishment would convert death penalty supporters spurred researchers to test his hypothesis empirically. Robert Bohm of the University of North Carolina is one researcher who has dedicated his career to studying the effects such knowledge has on death penalty opinion. From 1985 through 1989, he carefully measured the views of his students before and after a course devoted to the death penalty. The four-week class met five days a week to discuss the course text *Death Penalty in America*, to listen to presentations by Bohm and guest speakers, and to debate the issue.

Bohm's classes were composed primarily of criminal science majors and minors. At the beginning of the four-week period, Bohm gave his students a pretest to gauge their views on capital punishment and to measure their knowledge of the subject. That these pretests showed his students to be consistently uninformed or misinformed about the death penalty confirmed Marshall's belief that the public at large does not know very much about capital punishment. The pretests also showed that the students resembled the American public in their overwhelming support of the death penalty, ranging between 70 and 85 percent for the different classes. Some of the classes even demonstrated higher support than Gallup recorded for the American public during the same period. (Bohm, "Death Penalty Opinions: A Classroom Experience and Public Commitment," *Sociological Inquiry* 60, 1990.)

At the end of the course, the students took a posttest about their knowledge and attitudes. This test measured changes in knowledge levels about and support for the death penalty. Every time, Bohm found that support for the death penalty declined and opposition rose in his students by the end of the class, sometimes dramatically. For example, in 1986 the class began with 71 percent of the students in favor of the death penalty and 17 percent opposed. By the end of the class, only 39 percent of the class supported the death penalty, whereas 56 percent opposed it. Percentages varied from year to year, and only in 1986 did a majority of the class oppose the death penalty at the end, but there was always a trend toward declining support.

The students who changed their opinions usually had developed qualms about the administration of the death penalty. The reasons cited most often by students for a change in their views on the death penalty were racial discrimination and arbitrariness in the distribution of the death penalty, and the danger of executing innocent people. (Bohm, Vogel, and Maisto, "Knowledge and Death Penalty Opinion: A Panel Study," *Journal of Criminal Justice* 21, 1993.)

Professor Bohm identified an interesting phenomenon in his students as facts about the administration of the death penalty challenged their support of it. Very few of his students could simply live with the conflict. Some changed their opinion. But for every student who changed his mind about the death penalty, several classmates dug in and became stronger in their support of capital punishment. They resolved the conflict between their beliefs and what they were learning in class through a process Bohm called "biased assimilation." The students either attacked the validity of the material, misinterpreted the evidence to support their view, or espoused emotional, opinion-based foundations for their beliefs that were not subject to factual critique. For a lot of the students, usually more than half the class, the facts did not matter. Many of them simply interpreted and manipulated the facts to correspond to their beliefs. (Bohm and Vogel, "A Comparison of Factors Associated with Uninformed and Informed Death Penalty Opinions," *Journal of Criminal Justice* 22, 1994.)

As evidence for Justice Marshall's belief that support for the death penalty would evaporate once the American people knew the facts, Bohm's studies were decidedly mixed. Opposition to the use of capital punishment did increase with better knowledge, but seldom was there an absolute majority opposed, let alone the nearly complete opposition Marshall envisioned.

RACE AND PUBLIC OPINION

Justice Marshall would be further saddened by recent research into the links between race, racism, and support for the death penalty.

In over 50 years of Gallup polling, the African American community has opposed the death penalty in far greater numbers than has the white community. Traditionally, the difference in opinion has been explained by blacks' greater awareness of and sensitivity toward the racial discrimination inherent in the death penalty process.

Robert Young elaborated on the conventional explanation by attributing the diverging views to blacks' and whites' different relationships to the criminal justice system. He theorized that because blacks are more often the victims of crime and are also more often brought before the criminal justice system as defendants, they are more likely to be attuned to whether the system is administering justice in an evenhanded way. For African Americans the decision to support or not support the death penalty turns on whether they believe the system treats all its defendants fairly and equally.

Young described whites' relationship to the criminal justice system as more indirect and detached. The distance in the relationship causes whites to underestimate or entirely overlook the role of the administrators of justice and focus their attention instead on the individual criminals. According to Young, the determining factor for whites is their beliefs about the origins of crime. White opponents to the death penalty tend to at least partially attribute crime to environmental factors such as poverty and neglect. Those who believe criminals are wholly responsible for the choices they make are more likely to support the death penalty. (Young, "Race, Conceptions of Crime and Justice, and Support for the Death Penalty," *Social Psychology Quarterly* 54, 1991.)

Other researchers are less diplomatic about the reasons for racial disparities in opinion about the death penalty. In their studies, Steven Barkan and Steven Cohn blame racism pure and simple. Using data from the 1990 General Social Survey, they measured both white prejudice against African Americans and their support or opposition to the death penalty. In a special section devoted to attitudes about race, the survey asked respondents to indicate how strongly they would support or oppose living in a neighborhood that was half African American or having a relative or close family member marry an African American. It also measured antipathy toward African Americans by asking white respondents to rate on a seven-point scale their perceptions of blacks as lazy, unintelligent, desirous of living off welfare, unpatriotic, violent, and poor.

Comparing the information white respondents gave in the racial perceptions section to their views on the death penalty, Barkan and Cohn found a correlation between negative perceptions of blacks and support for the death penalty: "Simply put, many white people are both prejudiced against blacks and more likely to favor capital punishment." (Barkan and Cohn, "Racial Prejudice and Support for the Death Penalty by Whites," *Journal of Crime and Delinquency* 31, 1994.)

Today, it is socially unacceptable to be outwardly racist. I suppose this is progress: all but the most prejudiced and hate-filled feel uncomfortable publicly espousing racist ideologies. But this certainly does not mean that racism itself has gone away. Because racist attitudes are covert, they are more difficult to detect and fight. One must recognize and work through the code words that supporters of racist policies use in public discussions of such racially loaded issues as crime, welfare reform, teenage pregnancy, and affirmative action. Supporting the death penalty is one more way for some white Americans to strike out against African Americans and other minorities.

196

One of the most important lessons I've learned in my civil rights career is that we cannot legislate attitudes, opinions, and world views. We can only legislate behavior, and hope that, over time, the behavior will modify the attitudes. It is ethically unacceptable and legally unconstitutional to allow public policy to be based on racist viewpoints. Given the extent to which death penalty policy rests on public opinion, the racism inherent in that public opinion is one more reason why the death penalty must be eliminated.

THE SUPREME COURT: ONE EYE ON THE POLLS

We all know how public opinion affects our elected representatives. What is not so apparent, though, is how it affects the rulings of our courts. Routinely, judges take into consideration public opinion in how they control a trial and hand down sentences. Ironically, the case that laid the groundwork for the nation's highest court to consider popular opinion polls on capital punishment—the 1958 case *Trop v. Dulles*—didn't even pertain to the death penalty. Instead, it was about a native-born American who lost his citizenship due to his conviction by court-martial for wartime desertion. In this case, the Supreme Court ruled that revoking Trop's citizenship was a violation of the Eighth Amendment's ban on cruel and unusual punishment. In his opinion, Chief Justice Earl Warren wrote, "The

197

[Eighth] Amendment must draw its meaning from the evolving standards of decency that mark the progress of a maturing society."

Ten years later, in *Witherspoon v. Illinois* (1968), the Court cited Warren's "evolving standards" interpretation of the cruel and unusual ban to introduce public opinion polls into the death penalty debate. The *Witherspoon* decision stated that it was unconstitutional to keep potential jurors off a jury simply because they oppose the death penalty. Writing for the majority, Justice Potter Stewart cited 1966 Gallup poll figures that only 42 percent of Americans were in favor of the death penalty and 47 percent were opposed. Only six years before, proponents of capital punishment had been in the major- ity, but now Potter noted that a jury composed entirely of death penalty supporters would "speak only for a distinct and dwindling minority. (Bowers, "Capital Punishment and Contemporary Values: People's Misgivings and the Court's Misperceptions," *Law & Society Review* 27, 1993.)

In *Witherspoon*, the inclusion of public opinion polls worked for the opponents of the death penalty, but since then it has worked in favor of capital punishment's supporters. In 1972, when *Furman v. Georgia* temporarily invalidated capital punishment in the United States, Justice Marshall questioned the validity of an uninformed public's opinion, but in his dissenting opinion, Chief Justice Warren Burger pointed out that public opinion was shifting back toward the death penalty, with a 51 percent majority in favor in 1969 compared to only 42 percent in 1966.

When the question of whether the death penalty constitutes cruel and unusual punishment next came before the court in *Gregg v. Georgia*, the numbers were solidly on the side of death penalty supporters. The justices writing the opinion that reinstated capital punishment pointed to the 35 states that had written new death penalty statutes since *Furman* and the fact that juries were handing down death penalties under the new laws. Just as damning were polls taken in 1972 and 1973 showing that 57 and 59 percent of the public, respectively, supported the death penalty and that support was still growing. (Bowers, "Capital Punishment and Contemporary Values: People's Misgivings and the Court's Misperceptions")

A number of experts have suggested that the Court turned to vague, simplistic methods of gauging the public's opinion to avoid another damaging confrontation with the states. The memory of controversial decisions on school desegregation and other civil rights decisions was fresh in the collective mind of the Court, and unfortunately, the states most enraged by the Supreme Court's earlier decisions were also the strongest supporters of the death penalty. Hiding behind the *Witherspoon* principle gave the Court an easy way out of the moral and ethical question of whether the death penalty is cruel and unusual punishment.

Public opinion as measured by Gallup currently indi-

199

cates that support for the death penalty is somewhere between 75 and 80 percent. Given the precedent that has been set, the Court is unlikely to consider another challenge of the death penalty's constitutionality on the Eighth Amendment any time soon.

THE GOOD NEWS

That nearly eight out of ten Americans profess to Mr. Gallup that they support the death penalty might make the cause of eliminating capital punishment seem like an impossible mission. Public opinion polling, though, as we all know, is a tricky thing. In most cases, how a question is asked is actually more important than what question is asked.

Traditional surveys about capital punishment ask whether the respondent favors the death penalty for people found guilty of committing murder. Asking the question without putting it into a larger context may just be measuring the public's faith in the criminal justice system's effectiveness in fighting crime and protecting the public from dangerous criminals. In the words of Judge Charles Weltner of the Georgia Supreme Court, "Everybody believes that a person sentenced to life for murder will be walking the streets in seven years." If that is the case, and Americans believe that dangerous criminals who have killed and who, in their minds, may very well kill again will be back in their communities in a few years, then Americans might be "supporting" the death penalty out of fear and desperation. It feels like the only choice.

Recently the Death Penalty Information Center sponsored a survey to see how support for the death penalty might change if Americans were given a meaningful choice. The nonpartisan poll was conducted by Greenberg/Lake, a Democratic polling group, and the Tarrance Group, a Republican polling group. They found abstract support for the death penalty to be 77 percent, about the same as Gallup found. That number, however, fell when respondents were offered strict sentencing alternatives.

Given the choice between the death penalty and life imprisonment with no chance of parole for 25 years, support for the death penalty fell to 56 percent. Toughen the alternative to life imprisonment with no opportunity for parole, and support for the death penalty fell to a minority position—49 percent. When rigorous sentencing was combined with the inmate's working to pay restitution to the victim's family, support dropped even more. When respondents were given the choice between the death penalty or no parole for 25 years plus restitution, only 44 percent opted for the death penalty. When the alternative was no chance for parole plus restitution, even fewer, just 41 percent, supported capital punishment. (Dieter, *Sentencing for Life: Americans Embrace Alternatives to the Death Penalty*. Death Penalty Information Center, April 1993.)

These figures and other surveys done by the Death Penalty Information Center suggest that Americans have serious reservations about the death penalty and only pay

201

lip service to supporting it because they feel they have no choice. A number of aspects of the death penalty trouble respondents. Fifty-eight percent reported having either some or serious doubts about the death penalty because of the danger of executing innocent people. Forty-eight percent were troubled by racism in the distribution of the death penalty, and 46 percent were concerned by the high cost of capital punishment. Another 42 percent worried that the death penalty failed as a deterrent to other potential murders.

The missing link between an America that overwhelmingly supports the death penalty and an America that has grave ethical and practical doubts about its use is that most citizens believe life imprisonment really amounts to only a few years in jail—a relative slap on the wrist for a convicted murderer. In study after study, Americans woefully underestimate the time a convicted murderer will spend in jail. In New York, an amazing 25 percent of the people surveyed said that first degree murderers will spend less than 10 years in prison, and one out of two New Yorkers gave a number less than the state's bare minimum of 15 years. (Bowers, "Capital Punishment and Contemporary Values: People's Misgivings and the Court's Misperceptions.") Similar numbers are found in other states.

The truth is, however, that two-thirds of the states utilize sentencing that makes those convicted of first degree murder permanently ineligible for release, and most of the remaining states forbid parole consideration for a minimum of 25 years. (Dieter, *Sentencing for Life*.) Clearly, though, this is not common knowledge amongst the public, and it is the public that serves on capital juries. Most states that have the death penalty forbid judges, by law, to instruct juries what punishment would be handed down if they did not choose the death penalty. The so-called logic behind these statutes is that allowing judges to inform the jury about sentencing alternatives allows the possibility of biasing the jury, and that the particulars of the case—not the severity of the available alternatives—should decide whether the defendant receives the death penalty. One in four capital juries in Georgia interrupt their sentencing deliberation to ask the trial judge for further instruction. Ninety percent of the time their question is what the sentence would be if they did not choose the death penalty. Whatever the law's alleged intention, in an environment where jurors feel their decision in a gruesome murder case is between the death penalty and less than 10 years in prison, "gagging" the trial judge biases the process toward the death penalty. (Bowers, "Capital Punishment and Contemporary Values.")

Therefore, working to eliminate the death penalty through the Supreme Court and the Eighth Amendment may no longer be the most effective strategy. Our focus should shift to toughening sentencing alternatives in the few states in which they are lacking, publicizing those laws, and abolishing the judicial gag rule in capital cases. Maybe when the public, our nation's jury pool, again has confidence in non-capital sentencing and the alternatives to the death penalty are stringent and widely known, the death penalty will fall into disuse as juries opt for tough life imprisonment sentencing.

The research gauging public sentiment on capital punishment leads in divergent directions. On the one hand, opinion about the death penalty seems to be emotionally based, unresponsive to logic and reasoning, and at least partially based on racial hatred. Hardly encouraging news for a civil rights activist and death penalty opponent. Yet more in-depth surveys paint a picture of a citizenry ridden with doubt about the fairness and morality of the death penalty, but turning to it out of fear, ignorance, and desperation.

After careful reflection, I have concluded that there is at least an element of truth in each of the different findings on what is a very complex, difficult issue. I draw hope and strength from the evidence that America is receptive to alternatives to the death penalty, and I arm myself with the knowledge that the death penalty does stir up raw human emotion, not always of the purest origins.

In rereading Thurgood Marshall's opinion in the 1972 *Furman* decision, I am inspired and reinvigorated by his confidence in the American citizen:

> At a time in our history when the streets of the nation's cities inspire fear and despair, rather than pride and hope, it is difficult to maintain

objectivity and concern for our fellow citizens. But, the measure of a country's greatness is its ability to retain compassion in time of crisis. No nation in the recorded history of man has a greater tradition of revering justice and fair treatment for all its citizens in times of turmoil, confusion, and tension than ours. This is a country that clings to fundamental principles, cherishes its constitutional heritage, and rejects simple solutions that compromise the values that lie at the roots of our democratic system.

In striking down capital punishment, this Court does not malign our system of government. On the contrary, it pays homage to it. Only in a free society could right triumph in difficult times, and could civilization record its magnificent advancement. In recognizing the humanity of our fellow beings, we pay ourselves the highest tribute. We achieve "a major milestone in the long road up from barbarism" and join the approximately 70 other jurisdictions in the world which celebrate their regard for civilization and humanity by shunning capital punishment.

The righteous path blazed by Justice Marshall is the path of dignity and justice that has been followed by all other civilized nations of the world. It is time for the citizens of America to demand that our country turn onto that path, too.

APPENDIX

NATIONAL ORGANIZATIONS AGAINST THE DEATH PENALTY

American Civil Liberties Union
Capital Punishment Project
122 Maryland Avenue NE
Washington, DC 20002
202-675-2321

Amnesty International USA
Program to Abolish the Death Penalty
322 Eighth Avenue
New York, NY 10001
212-807-8400

Capital Punishment Research Project
PO Drawer 27
Headland, AL 36345
334-693-5225

Center for Constitutional Rights
666 Broadway, 7th Floor
New York, NY 10012
212-614-6464

CURE
PO Box 2310
Washington, DC 20013
202-789-2126

Death Penalty Information Center
1606 20th Street NW, 2nd Floor
Washington, DC 20009
202-347-2531

Death Row Support Project
PO Box 600
Liberty Mills, IN 46946
219-982-7480

Defense for Children International USA
30 Irving Place, 9th Floor
New York, NY 10003
212-228-4275

Feminists for Life of America
733 15th Street NW
Washington, DC 20005
202-737-3352

Friends Committee on National Legislation
245 Second Street NE
Washington, DC 20002
202-547-6000

Human Rights Watch
485 Fifth Avenue
New York, NY 10017
212-972-4013

Martin Luther King Center for Nonviolent Social Change
449 Auburn Avenue NE
Atlanta, GA 30312
404-524-1956

Murder Victims Families for Reconciliation
PO Box 208
Atlantic, VA 23303
804-824-0948

NAACP
4805 Mt. Hope Drive
Baltimore, MD 21215
410-358-3900

NAACP Legal Defense Fund
99 Hudson Street, 16th Floor
New York, NY 10013
212-219-1900

National Alliance Against Racist and Political Repression
11 John Street #702
New York, NY 10038
212-406-3330

National Association of Criminal Defense Lawyers
1627 K Street NW, 12th Floor
Washington, DC 20006
202-872-8688

National Association of Criminal Defense Lawyers
Death Penalty Committee
Roumain Building
343 Third Street, Suite 400
Baton Rouge, LA 70801
504-387-5786

National Bar Association
1225 11th Street NW
Washington, DC 20001
202-842-3900

National Black Police Association
3251 Mt. Pleasant Street NW, 2nd Floor
Washington, DC 20010
202-986-0410

National Coalition to Abolish the Death Penalty
918 F Street NW, Suite 601
Washington, DC 20004
202-347-2411

National Committee Against Repressive Legislation
3321 12th Street NE, 3rd Floor
Washington, DC 20017
202-529-4225

National Conference of Black Lawyers
1875 Connecticut Avenue NW, Suite 400
Washington, DC 20009
202-234-9735

National Conference on Crime and Delinquency
685 Market Street, #620
San Francisco, CA 94105
415-896-5109

National Execution Alert Network
918 F Street NW, Suite 601
Washington, DC 20004
202-347-2411

National Lawyers Guild
55 Sixth Avenue
New York, NY 10013
212-627-2656

National Legal Aid and Defender Association
1625 K Street NW, Suite 800
Washington, DC 20006
202-452-0620

National Urban League
500 East 62 Street
New York, NY 10021
212-310-9122

Partisan Defense Committee
PO Box 99
Canal Street Station
New York, NY 10013
212-406-4252

War Resister's League
339 Lafayette Street
New York, NY 10012
212-228-0450

SOURCES

Archer, Dane, Rosemary Gartner, and Marc Beittel, "Homicide and the Death Penalty: A Cross-National Test of a Deterrence Hypothesis." *Journal of Criminal Law and Criminology* 74, 1983.

Bailey, William. "Disaggregation in Deterrence and Death Penalty Research: The Case of Murder in Chicago." *Journal of Criminal Law and Criminology* 74, 1983.

Bailey, William and Ruth Peterson. "Police Killings and Capital Punishment: The Post-*Furman* Period." *Criminology* 25, 1987.

Barkan, Steven and Steven F. Cohn. "Racial Prejudice and Support for the Death Penalty by Whites." *Journal of Crime and Delinquency* 31, 1994.

Bohm, Robert. "Death Penalty Opinions: A Classroom Experience and Public Commitment." *Sociological Inquiry* 60, 1990.

Bohm, Robert, L. Clark, and A. Aveni. "Knowledge and Death Penalty Opinion: A Test of the Marshall Hypotheses." *Journal of Research in Crime and Delinquency* 18, 1991.

Bohm, Robert and Ronald Vogel. "A Comparison of Factors Associated with Uninformed and Informed Death Penalty Opinions." *Journal of Criminal Justice* 22, 1994.

Bohm, Robert, Ronald Vogel, and Albert A. Maisto. "Knowledge and Death Penalty Opinion: A Panel Study." *Journal of Criminal Justice* 21, 1993.

Bowers, William. "Capital Punishment and Contemporary Values: People's Misgivings and the Court's Misperceptions." *Law & Society Review* 27, 1993.

Bowers, William and Glenn Pierce. "Deterrence or Brutalization: What Is the Effect of Executions?" *Crime and Delinquency* 26, 1980.

Dicks, Shirley, ed. *Congregation of the Condemned: Voices Against the Death Penalty*. Prometheus Books, 1991.

Dieter, Richard. *Sentencing for Life: Americans Embrace Alternatives to the Death Penalty*. The Death Penalty Information Center, 1993.

Ellsworth, Phoebe and Samuel Gross. "Hardening of the Attitudes: Americans' Views on the Death Penalty." *Journal of Social Issues*, Summer 1994.

Gross, Samuel and Robert Mauro. *Death and Discrimination: Racial Disparities in Capital Sentencing*. Northeastern University, 1989.

Hansen, Mark. "Final Justice: Limiting Death Row Appeals." *ABA Journal*, March 1992.

Hood, Roger. *The Death Penalty: A World-Wide Perspective*. 1990.

Kronenwetter, Michael. *Capital Punishment: A Reference Handbook*. ABC-Clio, 1993

Lane, J. Mark. "Is There Life Without the Possibility of Parole? A Capital Defendant's Right to a Meaningful Alternative Sentence." *Loyola of Los Angeles Law Review* 26.

Lowell, Dodge. *Death Penalty Sentencing: Research Indicates Pattern of Racial Disparities*. U.S. General Accounting Office, 1990.

McFarland, Sam. "Is Capital Punishment a Short-Term Deterrent to Homicide? A Study of the Effects of Four

Recent American Executions." *Journal of Criminal Law and Criminology* 74, 1983.

Morgenthau, Robert. "What Prosecutors Won't Tell You." *New York Times*, February 7, 1995.

NAACP Legal Defense Fund. *Death Row, U.S.A.*

Quindlen, Anna. "The High Cost of Death." *New York Times*, November 19, 1994.

Rapaport, Elizabeth. "The Death Penalty and Gender Discrimination." *Law and Society Review* 25, 1991.

Reed, Emily Fabrycki. *The Penry Penalty: Capital Punishment and Offenders with Mental Retarda*tion. University Press of America, 1993.

Smolowe, Jill. "Race and the Death Penalty." *Time*, April 29, 1991.

U.S. Senate Committee on the Judiciary. *Innocence and the Death Penalty.* Hearing held April 1, 1993.

White, Welsh. *The Death Penalty in the Nineties: An Examination of the Modern System of Capital Punishment.* University of Michigan Press, 1991.

Young, Robert. "Race, Conceptions of Crime and Justice, and Support for the Death Penalty." *Social Psychology Quarterly* 54, 1991.

INDEX

217